May The Meditations of My Heart....

Olufemi Ijaodola

Drop-A-Line Publishing

OLUFEMI IJAODOLA

Unless otherwise indicated, all Scripture quotations are taken from the Holy Bible, New Living Translation, copyright © 1996, 2004, 2007, 2013, 2015 by Tyndale House Foundation. Used by permission of Tyndale House Publishers, Inc., Carol Stream, Illinois 60188. All rights reserved.

Scripture quotations marked NASB are taken from the New American Standard Bible®, Copyright © 1960, 1962, 1963, 1968, 1971, 1972, 1973, 1975, 1977, 1995 by The Lockman Foundation. Used by permission. (www.Lockman.org);

Scripture quotations marked NKJV are taken from the New King James Version® of the Bible. Copyright © 1982 by Thomas Nelson, Inc. Used by permission. All rights reserved;

Scripture quotations marked (NIV) are taken from the Holy Bible, New International Version®, NIV®. Copyright © 1973, 1978, 1984, 2011 by Biblica, Inc.™ Used by permission of Zondervan. All rights reserved worldwide. www.zondervan.com The "NIV" and "New International Version" are trademarks registered in the United States Patent and Trademark Office by Biblica, Inc.™;

Scripture quotations marked ESV are taken from the Holy Bible, English Standard Version® (ESV®), Copyright © 2001 by Crossway, a publishing ministry of Good News Publishers. All rights reserved;

The author has added capitals or italics to Scripture quotations as stated within for emphasis.

May The Meditations of My Heart…
Copyright © 2016 Olufemi Ijaodola
Illustrations copyright © 2016 Olufemi Ijaodola

All rights reserved. Except for brief excerpts, no part of this book may be reproduced or used in any form without the author's permission or consent.

ISBN: 978-0-9951841-0-7 (paperback edition)
ISBN: 978-0-9951841-1-4 (eBook edition)

Published by Drop-A-Line Publishing
Toronto, Canada

Print design, illustrations and cover layout:
Olufemi Ijaodola

Website:
www.dal-publishing.com

'May the words of my mouth and the meditations of my heart be pleasing unto You, O LORD, my Rock and Redeemer.'

- **Psalm 19:14**

OLUFEMI IJAODOLA

ACKNOWLEDGEMENTS

This book would never have been possible without the help of God, who inspires me and comforts me in my many failures. By His grace, all things have come together without too many setbacks.

A big thanks to all friends and family that have encouraged me over the years; you probably have little idea of how much God has used you in my life! A special thanks to those who helped me understand the little frustrations that rose up over this journey.

Thanks to my darling wife who encouraged (and challenged) me by the release of her own body of work. Thank you for also helping me bounce ideas off one another, and being my first reader!

A final thanks to you, reader, for acquiring a copy of this book; I doubt you have any idea of how encouraging it is that you did.

OLUFEMI IJAODOLA

PREFACE

Hello reader, I am grateful and pleased that you happened upon a copy of this book—be it by fate, luck, chance, or whatever you would call it—I personally believe it to be God's providence. I hope that if you have put your trust in the Lord Jesus Christ, you would be encouraged by this book all the more. If you have not, I hope its contents would give you some thought to consider the offer of hope and salvation that has been put before you. In either case, I pray this book might be of some help to you wherever you are in your walk in life.

This book is actually taken from a collection of emails that I sent to encourage my family and friends over the years. Over a period of time, it was suggested that the messages I shared would be great as a book. Perhaps I didn't pay as much attention to this suggestion as I should have, as it has taken me this long to get it done.

The idea has undergone some changes since then. It has grown from what I initially intended—a simple PDF giveaway—into a body of work I was inspired to make available to as many people as I possibly knew how to.

As you read, you might notice certain mannerisms or an informal style of writing. This would speak to how the original messages were set out. I tried to leave the content as unchanged as possible, except minor alterations and formatting. I felt like to start down a road of major changes for the sake of making them better would lead to no end, and so I would do well to leave them as they are, and pray the thoughts from back then are still as relevant as they were when I first wrote them down.

Please do not feel obligated to use the Bible versions I have made use of in this book; I used those that I felt were fitting (or spoke plainly) at the time of writing these meditations, but you are free to grab your Bible (if you have one) and read the passages in your usual version. If you do not have one however, the passages are already written out for your convenience.

I wouldn't call this a devotional book; maybe because it doesn't fit my idea of a daily devotional, or maybe because of the content itself. That being said, please feel free to read this book in any manner you wish; my only concern is your encouragement to walk with the Lord faithfully.

I am not a minister, preacher, or pastor, nor have I been to seminary or a bible college of any kind. I have no credential to speak of that makes me more qualified than another to render any specialist advice. I am simply a believer of Jesus Christ, like any other believer, leaning on grace and seeking His face and direction through prayer and His word, the holy Bible. However, I believe that the rendering godly advice is something every believer is able to do as we let the word of God abide in us, and we are renewed by our daily reading and study of it (Col. 3:16; Eph. 4:20-24; Rom. 12:1-2). We have the Holy Spirit that teaches us and leads us into all truth, and God the Father who grants wisdom and qualifies us for His good work (James 1:5; 2 Cor. 3:5-6), and so I do not believe that you have to be of a special office to offer some advice (although it is still your responsibility in regards to what kind of advice you give).

Although the word of God is inerrant, I am not, and I have probably already made some mistakes in the writing of this introduction alone. I do pray though, that my faults do not overshadow the blessing that I expect this book to be!

So, dear reader, do enjoy your read through. Feel free to pass this on to someone who you think might also benefit from it, and hopefully my words can be of some assistance to you as a fellow Christian, or simpler yet, a fellow pilgrim through life.

> 'Now may the God of hope fill you with all joy and peace in believing, that you may abound in hope by the power of the Holy Spirit.' – Romans 15:13, NASB

OLUFEMI IJAODOLA

Table of Contents

Meditations

The Living God	19
Treason	25
Joy in the Heart	33
The Guilty Set Free	43
The God You Serve	51
The Aftermath	59
Who is Truly Wise?	63
Reflections: A Meditation on Lessons of the Year	69
A Short Meditation on Proverbs 18:21	81
The Cost of Carrying Your Cross	85
Self-Examination	93
Habits & Motivations, Part 1	97
Habits & Motivations, Part 2	107
Who is Good?	123
Justice	129
Who Wants to Drink from a Dirty Spring?	133
Trifling Thrills and Precious Promises	139
The Weakness of My Heart	143

Social Death?	153
God Loves You Anyway	159
Don't Judge Me	163
The Challenger	173
To-Morrow	177
If You Have Been Raised Up…	181
Desires & Temptations	185

Poetry

A Restful Thought	197
Christ-Mass	199
Untitled	202
Maybe Someday	204
I'm Upset.	207
Get Behind Me	209
Nothing More	212
Are We There Yet?	214
Receive Us	218

MAY THE MEDITATIONS OF MY HEART…

OLUFEMI IJAODOLA

MAY THE MEDITATIONS OF MY HEART…

…To all truth seekers on this Incredible Walk…

OLUFEMI IJAODOLA

MAY THE MEDITATIONS OF MY HEART...

Meditations

OLUFEMI IJAODOLA

The Living God: A Short Meditation

I was reflecting on the greatness of our God—the one true living, everlasting One—and the futility of idolatry seems so stupid. Isaiah 44:6-20 puts it in perspective:

'This is what the LORD says—Israel's King and Redeemer, the LORD of Heaven's Armies:
"I am the First and the Last; there is no other God. Who is like Me? Let him step forward and prove to you his power. Let him do as I have done since ancient times when I established a people and explained its future.

Do not tremble; do not be afraid. Did I not proclaim My purposes for you long ago? You are My witnesses—is there any other God? No! There is no other Rock—not one!"

How foolish are those who manufacture idols. These prized objects are really worthless. The people who worship idols don't know this, so they are all put to shame. Who but a fool would make his own god—an idol that cannot help him one bit? All who worship idols will be disgraced along with all these craftsmen-mere humans-who claim they can make a god.
They may all stand together, but they will stand in terror and shame.

The blacksmith stands at his forge to make a sharp tool, pounding and shaping it with all his might. His work makes him hungry and weak. It makes him thirsty and faint.

Then the wood-carver measures a block of wood and draws a pattern on it. He works with chisel and plane and carves it into a human figure. He gives it human beauty and puts it in a little shrine. He cuts down cedars; he selects the cypress and the oak; he plants the pine in the forest to be nourished by the rain. Then he uses part of the wood to make a fire. With it he warms himself and bakes his bread. Then-yes, it's true-he takes the rest of it and makes himself a god to worship! He makes an idol and bows down in front of it!

He burns part of the tree to roast his meat and to keep himself warm. He says, "Ah, that fire feels good." Then he takes what's left and makes his god: a carved idol! He falls down in front of it, worshiping and praying to it. "Rescue me!" he says. "You are my god!" Such stupidity and ignorance! Their eyes are closed, and they cannot see. Their minds are shut, and they cannot think. The person who made the idol never stops to reflect, "Why, it's just a block of wood! I burned half of it for heat and used it to bake my bread and roast my meat. How can the rest of it be a god? Should I bow down to worship a piece of wood?"

The poor, deluded fool feeds on ashes. He trusts something that can't help him at all. Yet he cannot bring himself to ask, "Is this idol that I'm holding in my hand a lie?"'

...Unbelievable right?

...Yet a lot of us fall into the trap of idolatry, albeit not as obvious as this. We magnify things, people, circumstances and achievements—and sometimes even ourselves—above God, indirectly making it our god.

In the latter part of Colossians 3:5 it says, '...Don't be greedy, for a greedy person is an idolater, worshiping the things of this world.'
'Greed' here is also translated as 'covetousness'; we must be careful about the things we seek. We wouldn't normally think of our cravings for a particular thing to be a breach of the 1st commandment would we?

'"You must not have any other god but Me.' (Ex. 20:3)

Sometimes we get so caught up in what we're chasing after, thinking, "if only I had this" or "if only I was like that", "then my life would be better."

...But since when do we know what we need more than God? Do those things give life or secure our souls? Would getting that job make your salvation even more assured? Or does somehow 'lacking' this thing you crave, take away from the joy of your salvation? God forbid!

I have both an encouragement and an exhortation from Paul.

First, the encouragement, on how we should aspire to live:

'I know how to live on almost nothing or with everything. I have learned the secret of living in every situation, whether it is with a full stomach or empty, with plenty or little. For I can do everything through Christ, who gives me strength.' (Phil. 4:12-13)

Second, the exhortation, on how to be content:

'...Yet true godliness with contentment is itself great wealth. After all, we brought nothing with us when we came into the world, and we can't take anything with us when we leave it. So if we have enough food and clothing, let us be content.

But people who long to be rich fall into temptation and are trapped by many foolish and harmful desires that plunge them into ruin and destruction.' (1 Tim. 6:6-9)

Now, I'm not saying aspirations and dreams are bad, nor am I saying it is wrong to be inspired by successful people, but my ultimate word of caution would be to echo what John said:

'Dear children, keep away from anything that might take God's place in your hearts.' (1 John 5:21)

For remember, '...this world is fading away, along with everything that people crave. But anyone who does what pleases God will live forever.' (1 John 2:17)

...To end this on a good note so it's not all heavy-duty, check this out and see that the LORD takes care of His own (there are so many promises in the book of Proverbs alone):

Prov. 10:22 - 'The blessing of the LORD makes a person

rich, and He adds no sorrow with it.'

Prov. 13:25 - 'The godly eat to their hearts' content, but the belly of the wicked goes hungry.'

Prov. 10:3 - 'The LORD will not let the godly go hungry, but He refuses to satisfy the craving of the wicked.'

Prov. 14:11 - 'The house of the wicked will be destroyed, but the tent of the godly will flourish.'

Have a good day ^_^

Treason: A Short Meditation

After a heated night of swinging that Sword—shamefully passively, yet by some divine grace coming out victorious (let those who understand do so)—I started to ponder on the potency of sin.

As non-believers we were ruled by sin, governed by it, in love with it, and did not understand the gravity of our deeds:

Eph. 2:2 - 'You used to live in sin, just like the rest of the world, obeying the devil—the commander of the powers in the unseen world. He is the spirit at work in the hearts of those who refuse to obey God.'

Prov. 4:16 - 'For evil people can't sleep until they've done their evil deed for the day.
They can't rest until they've caused someone to stumble.'

Prov. 14:9 - 'Fools make fun of guilt, but the godly acknowledge it and seek reconciliation.'

Ps. 10:11 - 'The wicked think, "God isn't watching us! He has closed his eyes and won't even see what we do!"'

Gen. 6:5 - 'The LORD observed the extent of human wickedness on the earth, and He saw that everything they thought or imagined was consistently and totally evil.'

But as Christians—those who have been saved, we 'taste and see that the LORD is good', and we proclaim, 'Oh, the joys of those who take refuge in Him!' (Ps. 34:8).
Yes, we have been forgiven by Jesus the Christ who became our sin OFFERING (2 Cor. 5:21), and now we sing,

'Oh, what joy for those whose disobedience is forgiven, whose sin is put out of sight!
Yes, what joy for those whose record the LORD has cleared of guilt, whose lives are lived in complete honesty!' (Ps. 32:1-2)

However, although we have been made clean and right before God, we still have in-dwelling sin which is tethered to our corrupt and dying flesh (Rom. 7:22-24, Matt. 26:41).

But there is great news! Since Jesus died and was raised, sin's power over us was broken (Rom. 6:6-8), and so we are not ruled by our sin anymore:

'Sin is no longer your master, for you no longer live under the requirements of the law. Instead, you live under the freedom of God's grace.' (Rom. 6:14)

So now, we can fully enjoy a pursuit of righteousness, since sinning is now a CHOICE to the believer:

2 Tim. 2:22 - 'Run from anything that stimulates youthful lusts. Instead, pursue righteous living, faithfulness, love, and peace. Enjoy the companionship of those who call on the Lord with pure hearts.'

1 Cor. 10:13 - 'The temptations in your life are no different from what others experience. And God is faithful. He will not allow the temptation to be more than you can stand. When you are tempted, He will show you a way out so that you can endure.'

Heb. 4:16 - 'So let us come boldly to the throne of our gracious God. There we will receive His mercy, and we will find grace to help us when we need it most.'

...But then, why do we, as Christians, still sin... even though it's a CHOICE? Surely, since we are enlightened to our sinful condition PRE-Christ, and are enlightened to our glorious hope IN Christ, we would put to death our old ways and live in newness of life, and not WILLINGLY commit TREASON against our King?

Rom. 6:11-13 - 'So you also should consider yourselves to be dead to the power of sin and alive to God through Christ Jesus.
Do not let sin control the way you live; do not give in to sinful desires. Do not let any part of your body become an instrument of evil to serve sin. Instead, give yourselves completely to God, for you were dead, but now you have new life. So use your whole body as an instrument to do what is right for the glory of God.'

Eph. 4:17-24 - 'With the Lord's authority I say this: Live no longer as the Gentiles do, for they are hopelessly confused. Their minds are full of darkness; they wander far from the life God gives because they have closed their minds and hardened their hearts against Him.
They have no sense of shame. They live for lustful pleasure and eagerly practice every kind of impurity. But that isn't what you learned about Christ. Since you have heard about Jesus and have learned the truth that comes from Him, throw off your old sinful nature and your former way of life, which is corrupted by lust and deception.

Instead, let the Spirit renew your thoughts and attitudes. Put on your new nature, created to be like God—truly righteous and holy.'

1 John 3:4-6 - 'Everyone who sins is breaking God's law, for all sin is contrary to the law of God. And you know that Jesus came to take away our sins, and there is no sin in Him.
Anyone who continues to live in Him will not sin. But anyone who keeps on sinning does not know Him or understand who He is.'

Indeed, it's a sad state we're in :,(...but God is ever-gracious, ever-merciful, ever-faithful:

2 Tim. 2:13 - 'If we are unfaithful, He remains faithful, for He cannot deny who He is.'

BUT HE WILL NOT BE MOCKED!!

Col. 3:24-25 - 'Remember that the Lord will give you an inheritance as your reward, and that the Master you are serving is Christ.
But if you do what is wrong, you will be paid back for the wrong you have done. For God has no favorites.'

Gal. 6:7-8 - 'Don't be misled—you cannot mock the justice of God. You will always harvest what you plant. Those who live only to satisfy their own sinful nature will harvest decay and death from that sinful nature. But those who live to please the Spirit will harvest everlasting life from the Spirit.'

Prov. 15:10a - 'Whoever abandons the right path will be severely disciplined...'

1 John 3:7-9 - 'Dear children, don't let anyone deceive you about this: When people do what is right, it shows that they are righteous, even as Christ is righteous. But when people keep on sinning, it shows that they belong to the devil, who has been sinning since the beginning. But the Son of God came to destroy the works of the devil. Those who have been born into God's family do not make a practice of sinning, because God's life is in them. So they can't keep on sinning, because they are children of God.'

So, my brothers and sisters, this is just a short exhortation to you all (and to myself):

Rom. 8:12-13 - 'Therefore, dear brothers and sisters, you have no obligation to do what your sinful nature urges you to do. For if you live by its dictates, you will die. But if through the power of the Spirit you put to death the deeds of your sinful nature, you will live.'

1 Pet. 1:13-19 - 'So think clearly and exercise self-control. Look forward to the gracious salvation that will come to you when Jesus Christ is revealed to the world. So you must live as God's obedient children. Don't slip back into your old ways of living to satisfy your own desires. You didn't know any better then.
But now you must be holy in everything you do, just as God who chose you is holy. For the Scriptures say, "You must be holy because I am holy."
And remember that the heavenly Father to whom you pray has no favorites. He will judge or reward you according to what you do. So you must live in reverent fear of Him during your time as "foreigners in the land." For you know that God paid a ransom to save you from the empty life you inherited from your ancestors. And the ransom He paid was not mere gold or silver. It was the precious blood of Christ, the sinless, spotless Lamb of God.'

Phil. 2:12b-13 - '...Work hard to show the results of your salvation, obeying God with deep reverence and fear. For God is working in you, giving you the desire and the power to do what pleases Him.'

2 Pet. 1:10-11 - 'So, dear brothers and sisters, work hard to prove that you really are among those God has called and chosen. Do these things, and you will never fall away. Then God will give you a grand entrance into the eternal Kingdom of our Lord and Savior Jesus Christ.'

Ps. 119:9 - 'How can a young person stay pure? By obeying Your word.'

Even though I didn't go too in-depth with this, I hope you were edified nonetheless. Please feel free to hit me up and we can chop this up some more if you want!

Joy in the Heart: A Short Meditation

I woke up in the wee hours of the night/morning with a weighty reverence for God and how great He is, and psalm 16:7 came to mind:

'I will bless the LORD who guides me; even at night my heart instructs me.'

Meditating on what He's done for me, I remembered a song I heard a while back:

"How could I repay such a debt, except with my life?
How could I give anything but sacrifice?
Sacrifice of praise...
To the King, eternal, immortal;
Be all the glory, forever, amen.
To the King, eternal, immortal;
Be all the glory, forever, amen." (Natalie Grant, 'Song to the King')

Just being in awe of Him put it all in perspective—my life, my purpose, my trials, my failures, my successes—all secondary in light of Him.

So I proceeded to do what was the only reasonable,

acceptable, and rightful response to such awesomeness: Praised and worshiped the one true living God!

However, one thing started becoming apparent to me... How woefully we fail as Christians.

Sure, in our days of unbelief we did many questionable things in our lives, and after coming to Christ, we have tasted and seen that the LORD is good. Yet, as if slave to some twisted disposition, like dogs we return to our vomit. We still sin. I don't get it. I mean, I get it... But I don't get it. I mean, I get it—it's indwelling sin—but I mean, I don't GET IT, it's so stupid. We're so stupid.

How wretched we truly are! I think of scriptures like, '...Because we have these promises, dear friends, let us cleanse ourselves from everything that can defile our body or spirit. And let us work toward complete holiness because we fear God' (2 Cor. 7:1), and I wonder, how shallow does our love for God run? I mean, we confess that we love Him and that He's our lord, but then if we love Him, wouldn't we love what He loves (righteousness, justice, holiness, godliness, etc.) and hate what He hates (sin, wickedness, evil, etc.)?

We can confess with our lips all we want, but if our hearts' true confession is contrary, then our words hold no weight.

John writes: 'If someone claims, "I know God," but doesn't obey God's commandments, that person is a liar and is not living in the truth.' (1 John 2:4)

And Jesus himself said, '"If you love Me, obey My commandments.' (John 14:15)

And we know that '...all sin is contrary to the law of God' (1 John 3:4), so when we sin, we show that we do not love Him, or at least, not more than the fleeting pleasures we get from sinning:

'But those who obey God's word truly show how completely they love Him. That is how we know we are living in Him.' (1 John 2:5)

So then, I admit, I started despairing a bit. I mean, I say I love God, and I believe I do, but I can't go on sinning and say "oh, it's indwelling sin, it's not my fault," and quote

Paul and say, "I am not the one doing wrong; it is sin living in me that does it."

As I drifted from my highs to my lows, this beautiful passage came to mind:

'The LORD is compassionate and merciful, slow to get angry and filled with unfailing love. He will not constantly accuse us, nor remain angry forever. He does not punish us for all our sins; He does not deal harshly with us, as we deserve. For His unfailing love toward those who fear Him is as great as the height of the heavens above the earth. He has removed our sins as far from us as the east is from the west.

The LORD is like a father to His children, tender and compassionate to those who fear Him. For He knows how weak we are; He remembers we are only dust. Our days on earth are like grass; like wildflowers, we bloom and die. The wind blows, and we are gone—as though we had never been here. But the love of the LORD remains forever with those who fear Him. His salvation extends to the children's children of those who are faithful to His covenant, of those who obey His commandments!' **(Ps. 103:8-18)**

He knows how weak I am! He knew how weak I would be! His salvation, His love, was NEVER dependent on me in the first place! Jesus didn't come down to strike a deal with me, saying He will offer me salvation if, and only if, I offer Him my unrelenting faithfulness... NO!

He came to offer me salvation, and as a result, I strive to offer Him my unrelenting faithfulness, and even when I fail (woefully, like, let's not even go there :/), He tells me I'm forgiven, and I should trust Him and keep striving.

Paul wrote to the Philippians: '...I press on to possess that perfection for which Christ Jesus first possessed me.' (Phil. 3:12b)

And so this is what we must do: '...And so, dear brothers and sisters, I plead with you to give your bodies to God because of all He has done for you. Let them be a living and holy sacrifice—the kind He will find acceptable. This is truly the way to worship Him.' (Rom. 12:1)

I thought about why we easily fall into sin, and identified some points to share quickly (please bear in mind how interrelated these points are):

1) We read the Word of God nowhere nearly as much as we ought to.

The psalmist wrote: 'How can a young person stay pure? By obeying Your word.' (Ps. 119:9)

Jesus said when the Word abides in you, you will bear fruit. We buy into the empty promises of sin because we forget all the glorious promises of God that have been fulfilled in Christ.

Our warfare against sin and temptation is not carnal, but spiritual. We must kill the sin in us by the Spirit (Rom. 8:13), but how can we go to war without the ONLY weapon we have? (Eph. 6:17)

2) We meditate on God nowhere nearly as much as we ought to.

Peter writes: 'By His divine power, God has given us everything we need for living a godly life. We have received all of this by coming to know Him, the one who called us to Himself by means of His marvelous glory and excellence.

And because of His glory and excellence, He has given us

great and precious promises. These are the promises that enable you to share His divine nature and escape the world's corruption caused by human desires.' **(2 Pet. 1:3-4)**

Paul writes: 'Since you have been raised to new life with Christ, set your sights on the realities of heaven, where Christ sits in the place of honor at God's right hand. Think about the things of heaven, not the things of earth. For you died to this life, and your real life is hidden with Christ in God.' **(Col. 3:1-3)**

John writes: 'Dear children, keep away from anything that might take God's place in your hearts.' **(1 John 5:21)**

Simply put, when we behold God and Christ our Savior more and more, everything is put in perspective. As we grow in our knowledge of Him, we become more realistic in our life view.

Some might find it funny that I say 'realistic', but tell me this:

Who would, after knowing that they were not made to be satisfied with this world, but rather were made for an eternal life in never-ending satisfaction and fellowship with the biggest thing—literally and metaphorically—in this universe, still choose to chase the fleeting passions of this dying world? (1 John 2:15-17)

Surely, not someone who was being realistic!

3) We pray nowhere nearly as much as we ought to.

Constant fellowship with God is always good (1 Thess. 5:17), but it shouldn't take the place of us setting aside proper times for prayer (Matt. 26:41, Heb. 4:16). Fighting temptation and slaying indwelling sin is a tough 24/7 lifetime job. No breaks. We CANNOT do this in our own strength. Mini-whispered prayers are cool, but we must set aside time to PRESS IN.

So you see the issue? We do not pray and fellowship with our God as we ought to.

Why not?

Because we do not know and savor our God as we ought to.

Why not?

Because we do not read His Word and revelation as we ought to!

So I exhort you all today, to '...work hard to show the results of your salvation, obeying God with deep reverence and fear', knowing that '...God, who began the good work within you, will continue His work until it is finally finished on the day when Christ Jesus returns.' (Phil. 2:12, Phil. 1:6)

Have a blessed day! ^_^

OLUFEMI IJAODOLA

The Guilty Set Free: A Short Meditation

I had a very peculiar dream last night. I mean, usually my dreams are pretty outlandish; saving the world or being the hero was all in the day's job (or night job, I should say). However, last night's dream was quite peculiar indeed.

I dreamt that I was in a classroom studying, when all of a sudden three guards walked in and called my name. I had nothing to hide so I stood up, and they said I was under arrest! I was like, "waaaa?!" (as you can probably imagine), and I wasn't even told my crime or charge.

I was dragged out of the classroom and we proceeded to walk down this long hallway, where they told me I was to be—get this—crucified!

Now, normally I would think I'd go on to protest against my execution, especially if I didn't know what I did that warranted such an extreme punishment, but the argument I voiced out the most as I fell to my knees was this:

'Please don't kill me the same way my Lord died!' (Note: I heard the Apostle Peter made such an objection at his martyrdom)

Now that surprised me...

But the guards didn't care, they carried on taking me to the execution grounds, and I looked out into the courtyard and saw three poles, with the middle pole vacant just for me.
Now this time I fell flat on my face, praying to God, asking Him that if I must die the same way my Lord did, may He make me worthy, and that may my death be pleasing unto Him...

That surprised me even more...

So there I was, lying on the wooden beam they were going to nail my wrists to. I had resigned myself to my fate. All of a sudden someone approached, knocked out the guards (haha yes, yes, I know), and told me I was free to leave... I ran outta there grinning from ear to ear, with this unexplainable joy! I was free! Those who saw me marveled, for they thought me dead! My life was a living testimony, and oh, what a testimony it was!

Okay... What a dream, right?

When I thought about it, I remembered that we had been discussing the story of Barabbas in my youth class the day before. The discussion was about how we could see glimpses of ourselves in that story, and how the innocent got crucified and the guilty got set free... The dream seemed to make more sense.

However, that wasn't entirely the situation in the dream. I was NOT Barabbas, and my acknowledgment and confession of Jesus as my Lord showed that I was saved (ergo Christ had ALREADY taken my place on the cross), so it made the whole thing even more intriguing.

I will not begin an open discussion about what the dream could have meant, but I will acknowledge two significant points arising in the dream:

1) The boldness and faith to lay your life down for God

The dream 'me', although not knowing his crime (but as I was saved, I would like to assume that my crime must have been nothing other than my faith <1 Pet. 4:14-16>), was prepared to lay his life down for his faith. He prayed that his suffering/death would be pleasing to God!

1 Pet. 4:1-2 - 'So then, since Christ suffered physical pain, you must arm yourselves with the same attitude He had, and be ready to suffer, too. For if you have suffered physically for Christ, you have finished with sin. You won't spend the rest of your lives chasing your own desires, but you will be anxious to do the will of God.'

1 Pet. 4:19 - 'So if you are suffering in a manner that pleases God, keep on doing what is right, and trust your lives to the God who created you, for He will never fail you.'

Oh how I pray for such confidence for all my brothers and sisters (and myself), that we would be willing to give up our lives for Christ!

Jesus said, 'If you try to hang on to your life, you will lose it. But if you give up your life for My sake and for the sake of the Good News, you will save it.' **(Mark 8:35)**

And Paul wrote: 'For I fully expect and hope that I will never be ashamed, but that I will continue to be bold for Christ, as I have been in the past. And I trust that my life will bring honor to Christ, whether I live or die. For to me, living means living for Christ, and dying is even better.' (Phil. 1:20-21)

2) The joy of Salvation

The dream 'me' did not die that day, and he was made free to proclaim the greatness of God, and to be a witness to people. How amazing is that?!

Today, I was taking a look at Proverbs 15:30 and it says:

'A cheerful look brings joy to the heart; good news makes for good health.'

Good news gladdens the heart by illuminating truth and providing great joy. A glad heart in turn is reflected in our composition (Prov. 15:13a), and also brings us peace in our being (Prov. 14:30a). Our joy comes from our hope, and our hope comes from God. And it is indeed good news what Christ has done for us!

The psalmist David writes in Ps. 16:9-11 - 'No wonder my heart is glad, and I rejoice. My body rests in safety. For you will not leave my soul among the dead or allow Your holy one to rot in the grave. You will show me the way of life, granting me the joy of Your presence and the pleasures of living with You forever.'

'Holy one' in this passage also refers to Christ, who as we know, rose on the third day, just like the Scriptures prophesied.

This is good news! To the unbeliever, it means that salvation is possible for all those who put their trust in Jesus. To the believer, it means that salvation is promised for all those who put their trust in Jesus.

We were set free, for God, in His just mercies, 'made Christ, who never sinned, to be the offering for our sin, so that we could be made right with God through Christ.' (2 Cor. 5:21). Christ took OUR place on that cross. He bore upon Himself our punishment and our curse.

'Christ has rescued us from the curse pronounced by the law. When He was hung on the cross, He took upon Himself the curse for our wrongdoing. For it is written in the Scriptures, "Cursed is everyone who is hung on a tree."' (Gal. 3:13)

Our freedom is our testimony to all, that God is so merciful and loving, that He saved us! And for every moment we're alive, we have the duty, nay, the privilege, to display God's goodness and tell those who we can that salvation is here.

I want to leave you all with this amazing verse; I hope you meditate on it and that the Holy Spirit teaches you the wealth of truth in it:

Gal. 2:20 - 'My old self has been crucified with Christ. It is no longer I who live, but Christ lives in me. So I live in this earthly body by trusting in the Son of God, who loved me and gave Himself for me.'

Have a blessed day ^_^

OLUFEMI IJAODOLA

The God You Serve: A Short Meditation

A question crossed my mind a couple of years ago, and resurfaced recently. I thought I might as well extend the question to you all:

Who is the God you serve?

Sounds simple right? And yet, not quite so.

This meditation is a meditation about idolatry, albeit the subtle, dangerously potent type. Sure, bowing down to statues is definitely a no-no, and self-gratification is nothing but folly, but an even deeper trap of idolatry that <u>a lot</u> of professing Christians fall into is the trap of worshiping a false god.

Now that sounds whack right? But it's true. A lot of us believe we are serving the true God, when actually we are serving idols, created in our minds by cause of our sinful depravity and biblical negligence.

I came across a saying a while back, and although I don't remember exactly what was said, it went something like:

"If they are comfortable and not offended or convicted by

the God they serve, then odds are that they are not serving the God of Scripture."

I found that quite interesting; The reason a lot of people (and you would soon notice this especially when you evangelize to people, but sadly also when speaking to some within the fellowship of Christ) don't see the urgency of repentance, the potency of sin, or lack a reverent fear of God is because they have created an idea or image of God in their minds which allows them to live the way they choose, while still assuring them of heaven!

"I've never killed anyone."
"I'm a good person."
"I go to church."
"God sees my heart; you can't judge me."
"God is loving; he wouldn't just send me to hell."

The protest goes on. By subconsciously (or consciously) taking up different views and opinions about God, we have created this 'God' in our minds, who acts the way we want him to, and even though we sin, it's okay, because we go to church, or because our parents do so

So, I ask again: who is this 'God' you serve? Is it the God I say? Or the God your friends/peers say? Or the God your pastor preaches about? Or the God who revealed Himself in His Word, the holy Bible?

Who will tell us who the true living God is? Whose testimony can we believe? Who will speak of the attributes of God? Who will learn us in the ways of the all-powerful, highly lifted up, eternal One?

During Moses' encounter with God, he asked:

'..."If I go to the people of Israel and tell them, 'The God of your ancestors has sent me to you,' they will ask me, 'What is his name?' Then what should I tell them?" God replied to Moses, "I AM WHO I AM. Say this to the people of Israel: I AM has sent me to you."
God also said to Moses, "Say this to the people of Israel: Yahweh, the God of your ancestors—the God of Abraham, the God of Isaac, and the God of Jacob—has sent me to you.
This is My eternal name, My name to remember for all generations.' **(Ex. 3:13-15)**

Amazing right? God also revealed Himself to His people:

'The LORD gives righteousness and justice to all who are treated unfairly. He revealed His character to Moses and His deeds to the people of Israel.' **(Ps. 103:6-7)**

I mean, He even declared His attributes to Moses:

'...Then the LORD came down in a cloud and stood there with him; and He called out His own name, Yahweh. The LORD passed in front of Moses, calling out,
"Yahweh! The LORD! The God of compassion and mercy! I am slow to anger and filled with unfailing love and faithfulness. I lavish unfailing love to a thousand generations. I forgive iniquity, rebellion, and sin. But I do not excuse the guilty. I lay the sins of the parents upon their children and grandchildren; the entire family is affected—even children in the third and fourth generations."' **(Ex. 34:5-7)**

The Word of God is God's testimony of Himself, His revelation of His glory to all of mankind. His amazing acts and His fulfillment of promises, His just judgments and His undeserved mercies, His overwhelming grace and His fierce wrath; it's all recorded for the purpose of our illumination.

The psalmist writes: '...the testimony of the Lord is sure, making wise the simple' **(Ps. 19:7, ESV)**

Hebrews 1:1-2 says, 'Long ago God spoke many times and in many ways to our ancestors through the prophets. And now in these final days, He has spoken to us through His Son. God promised everything to the Son as an inheritance, and through the Son He created the universe.'

God does not need to raise up prophets to speak to us anymore; His Word is complete for our instruction. His testimony is trustworthy for our faith. His revelation is enough for our hope.

Paul wrote in his second letter to Timothy:

'You have been taught the holy Scriptures from childhood, and they have given you the wisdom to receive the salvation that comes by trusting in Christ Jesus.
All Scripture is inspired by God and is useful to teach us what is true and to make us realize what is wrong in our lives. It corrects us when we are wrong and teaches us to do what is right. God uses it to prepare and equip His people to do every good work.' **(2 Tim. 3:15-17)**

The highest authority we have on earth pertaining to our incredible walk of faith is the Word of God (which is why we need to read and study it daily for the renewal of our minds! <Rom. 12:2>); and so it only makes sense that we should rely on the Word of God to know who God is.

(Note: To those who might want to object by bringing up the works of the Holy Spirit: we know that He does not say/do anything contrary to what the Scripture teaches; God is not divided <see John 14:26, John 15:26, John 16:13-15>).

Jesus puts it in a better way Himself when He says, "'My Father has entrusted everything to Me. No one truly knows the Son except the Father, and no one truly knows the Father except the Son and those to whom the Son chooses to reveal Him.'" (Matt. 11:27)

I think the point I'm trying to make is simply put across by John when he writes in 1 John. 5:9,

'Since we believe human testimony, surely we can believe the greater testimony that comes from God. And God has testified about His Son.'

Who better to speak about God but God Himself?

So, I exhort you all, let's not get caught up in our modern-day idolatry by creating a more comfortable version of God to worship, because God makes it VERY clear: '"You must not have any other god but Me.' (Ex. 20:3).

We are convicted when we go before the true living God revealed in Scripture, and rightly so! For we are being sanctified (made holy) and transformed into the likeness of God; truly righteous and holy (Eph. 4:23-24, 1 Pet. 1:16).

The Aftermath: A Short Meditation

Just a quick thought to ponder on:

Each time you fall to temptation, you're not only sinning against the eternal Holy One, but you're 'sowing' to the flesh; planting seeds in your flesh leads to death, and cultivates a habit that makes it harder to pursue righteousness.

Anyone who has put their trust in Christ Jesus is under no obligation to sin. Therefore, dear Christian, before you make that CHOICE to sin, remember that even though there is no condemnation for those in Christ, there are repercussions for your actions. Oh, that we would be sober-minded and consider our actions better!

Rom. 8:5-6 - 'Those who are dominated by the sinful nature think about sinful things, but those who are controlled by the Holy Spirit think about things that please the Spirit. So letting your sinful nature control your mind leads to death. But letting the Spirit control your mind leads to life and peace.'

Gal. 6:8 - 'Those who live only to satisfy their own sinful nature will harvest decay and death from that sinful nature. But those who live to please the Spirit will harvest everlasting life from the Spirit.'

1 John 3:9 - 'Those who have been born into God's family do not make a practice of sinning, because God's life is in them. So they can't keep on sinning, because they are children of God.'

1 Cor. 11:32 - '...Yet when we are judged by the Lord, we are being disciplined so that we will not be condemned along with the world.'

1 Pet. 1:13-17 - '...So think clearly and exercise self-control. Look forward to the gracious salvation that will come to you when Jesus Christ is revealed to the world. So you must live as God's obedient children.
Don't slip back into your old ways of living to satisfy your own desires. You didn't know any better then. But now you must be holy in everything you do, just as God who chose you is holy. For the Scriptures say, "You must be holy because I am holy."
And remember that the heavenly Father to whom you pray has no favorites. He will judge or reward you according to what you do. So you must live in reverent fear of Him during your time as "foreigners in the land."'

Ps. 119:9, v11 - 'How can a young person stay pure? By obeying Your word... I have hidden Your word in my heart, that I might not sin against You.'

2 Pet. 1:10 - 'So, dear brothers and sisters, work hard to prove that you really are among those God has called and chosen. Do these things, and you will never fall away.'

Be encouraged brethren ^_^

Who Is Truly Wise?: A Short Meditation

I've been thinking about what happened in my youth class at one of our meetings... Our session ended with a climatic debate about the relativity of truth.

Of course, we know that the flagship thought for endorsing this ideology is religion; "I believe what I believe, you believe what you believe. What is true for me is not necessarily true for you."

Now, even from a logical standpoint, the statement is flawed, as truth has to be objective and constant by nature, ergo it cannot be subjective and change depending on the individual's perspective.

During this debate, I found myself trying to explain how flawed such a logic is, and I think I missed the whole point of what was happening.

We all knew that the underlying issue of the debate was whether one could actually profess that Jesus is the ONLY way and the ONLY truth, and that all others were lies and false (this was the topic of the youth class session, and yes Jesus is, see John 14:6 <and the Church says, "amen">).

After all, we live in a society and culture of mathematical equations and the need for facts to prove truth, so anything in that 'grey area' is relative. So, in my quest to use logic to show the folly in such a statement, I felt like I missed the point.

When the dust settled, I remembered this passage:

'The message of the cross is foolish to those who are headed for destruction! But we who are being saved know it is the very power of God. As the Scriptures say, "I will destroy the wisdom of the wise and discard the intelligence of the intelligent."

So where does this leave the philosophers, the scholars, and the world's brilliant debaters? God has made the wisdom of this world look foolish. Since God in His wisdom saw to it that the world would never know Him through human wisdom, He has used our foolish preaching to save those who believe. It is foolish to the Jews, who ask for signs from heaven. And it is foolish to the Greeks, who seek human wisdom. So when we preach that Christ was crucified, the Jews are offended and the Gentiles say it's all nonsense.

But to those called by God to salvation, both Jews and Gentiles, Christ is the power of God and the wisdom of God.' (1 Cor. 1:18-24)

The passage, written so long ago, clearly captures the two main opposing camps of faith in Christ today: those who walk by sight (seeking signs and miracles, "seeing is believing"), and those who walk by logic ("where is your proof? What is your evidence?")

Since none seek after God by their own will (Rom. 3:10-13, John 6:44), should we be surprised by this?

When faced with such adversity by those who try and say Christianity is foolishness, I suppose the rational and prompt response is to defend the faith, right? (2 Tim. 4:7, 1 Pet. 3:15)
But what we often do is try and use the same rationale they try to attack our Faith with to defend it. While that is admirable (and I'm not saying it's a bad thing), we must remember that God's salvation plan does NOT fit in with human wisdom, nor can it be explained by it.
Paul writes to the Corinthian church:

'When I first came to you, dear brothers and sisters, I didn't use lofty words and impressive wisdom to tell you God's secret plan. For I decided that while I was with you

I would forget everything except Jesus Christ, the one who was crucified. I came to you in weakness-timid and trembling. And my message and my preaching were very plain. Rather than using clever and persuasive speeches, I relied only on the power of the Holy Spirit. I did this so you would trust not in human wisdom but in the power of God.' (1 Cor. 2:1-5)

Trying to portray the gospel of Jesus Christ from a human point of view is not the best of starts. Paul sheds some more light on this in the next chapter:

'No one can know a person's thoughts except that person's own spirit, and no one can know God's thoughts except God's own Spirit. And we have received God's Spirit (not the world's spirit), so we can know the wonderful things God has freely given us.
When we tell you these things, we do not use words that come from human wisdom. Instead, we speak words given to us by the Spirit, using the Spirit's words to explain spiritual truths. But people who aren't spiritual can't receive these truths from God's Spirit. It all sounds foolish to them and they can't understand it, for only those who are spiritual can understand what the Spirit means.' (1 Cor. 2:11-14)

Don't get me wrong, I'm not saying there is no need for apologetics. What I am saying is that NO ONE can come to the knowledge of Christ based on THEIR OWN wisdom:

1 Cor. 3:18-20 - 'Stop deceiving yourselves. If you think you are wise by this world's standards, you need to become a fool to be truly wise. For the wisdom of this world is foolishness to God. As the Scriptures say, "He traps the wise in the snare of their own cleverness." And again, "The LORD knows the thoughts of the wise; He knows they are worthless."'

Rom. 1:22 - '...Claiming to be wise, they instead became utter fools.'

We must remember that salvation is a spiritual matter; revealed by the Spirit, received by the Spirit, and realized by the Spirit « there are no grounds for human wisdom in that.

So, reflecting on all these things, I think of Paul's letters to Timothy:

'Timothy, guard what God has entrusted to you. Avoid godless, foolish discussions with those who oppose you with their so-called knowledge.' (1 Tim. 6:20)

'Again I say, don't get involved in foolish, ignorant arguments that only start fights. A servant of the Lord must not quarrel but must be kind to everyone, be able to teach, and be patient with difficult people. Gently instruct those who oppose the truth. Perhaps God will change those people's hearts, and they will learn the truth.
Then they will come to their senses and escape from the devil's trap. For they have been held captive by him to do whatever he wants.' (2 Tim. 2:23-26)

I hope this meditation has been edifying and encouraging. As we're talking about wisdom, it only seems fitting that I should leave you all with a proverb:

Prov. 3:5-7 - 'Trust in the LORD with all your heart; do not depend on your own understanding. Seek His will in all you do, and He will show you which path to take. Don't be impressed with your own wisdom. Instead, fear the LORD and turn away from evil.'

Reflections: A Meditation on Lessons of the Year

With today being the end of the year, I thought I would take a moment and reflect on some of the things I've learnt this year, and below are 10 of the things that came to mind most. I'm just as guilty as any about these points, so I do not claim otherwise, but I felt it might encourage you as it did me.

What Have I Learnt?

- **<u>Jesus is Lord</u>**; One with the Father and the Spirit, wrapped in flesh to atone for sin, and is seated at the right hand of the Father till all His enemies are humbled under His feet, and He reveals His eternal kingdom to all the earth. HalleluYah! (Phil. 2:5-11, Col. 3:1-4)

All things are in His hands, and we might not understand why certain things happen the way they do, but we do know that 'from Him and through Him and to Him are all things. To Him be glory forever. Amen.' **(Rom. 11:36, ESV)**

- **It is a human fault, to always find fault in everything;** Ungratefulness is a chain we find hard to rid of.

When things are going well, we either find it too good to be true, or think it is perhaps due to our own excellence.

When things are not going well, we grumble and complain like it is perhaps some form of moral injustice that we would be subjected to such.

When things are neither exceptional nor bad, we are tempted to groan at the uneventful moments, rather than being thankful for a season of calm reflection. (Ecc. 7:14, 1 Thess. 5:18)

- **Lust is a BEAST;** Oh how many a times have I put myself at the mercy of the depraved beast that not only seeks to drag me down into the abyss, but transforms and grows more depraved every time I succumb to its calling, making it even harder to fight off.

In Hebrews chapter 11 God draws our attention to some of the Saints of Old, and then encourages us not to grow weary but to 'strip off every weight that slows us down, especially the sin that so easily trips us up.' (**Heb. 12:1**) And how do we do this? I shall share the secret:

Heb. 12:2 - 'We do this by keeping our eyes on Jesus, the champion who initiates and perfects our faith. Because of the joy awaiting Him, He endured the cross, disregarding its shame. Now He is seated in the place of honor beside God's throne.'

Col. 3:2-3 - 'Think about the things of heaven, not the things of earth. For you died to this life, and your real life is hidden with Christ in God.'

- <u>Pride, the silent but deadly sin</u>; There is so much to be said about the sin of pride. The cause of a third of heaven to be cast down along with that great adversary of mankind, Satan (Isa. 14:12-16, Eze. 28:11-17). If such angelic beings, better than you and I, were subjected to such, we are surely not exempt.

Pride is the sin that produces other sin. Pride in our self-worth hinders our subjection to God and our accountability for our actions, leading to idolatry.

It encourages self-centered behavior and therefore rejects the command to love our neighbors.

It promotes self-satisfaction and so disregards the principle of honoring the opposite sex, in the quest to indulge in sexual immorality. The list goes on and on.

Perhaps the most dangerous aspect of this sin is how silent it can be, how easily it can go under the radar, how harmless it can seem. God warns us not to take pride in ourselves, and to boast only in the LORD (Jer. 9:23-24, 1 Cor. 1:31, Prov. 3:34, Prov. 11:2, Prov. 18:12).

- **We MUST perfect holiness;** In our culture of compromise and relativity, it comes as no surprise that the continuous war against in-dwelling sin is quickly forgotten, and sanctification is paid no real thought. Christianity has been contextualized to the point of being irrelevant. A thirst for holiness is seen as too religious, and a practice of righteousness is labelled overkill, even by those in the Church.

How tightly have we let our enemy veil the truth from our

eyes? If we gave just a moment to search the Scriptures, we would quickly find how adamant and passionate God is about holiness! He judged the world once because of it (Gen. 6:5-6, 7:4), and He will once again (Eph. 5:5-8).

If the result of sin is death and eternal separation from God (Rom. 6:23, Rev. 20:11-15), and if the extent of the depravity of sin is so deep and costly that God humbled Himself in the form of man so He might die and shed His blood for our atonement (2 Cor. 5:21, Heb. 9:22-28), why do we persist in taking it lightly, especially after learning the truth of this?

God demands, 'You must be holy because I am holy.' (1 Pet. 1:15), **and the apostle exhorts,** 'let us cleanse ourselves from everything that can defile our body or spirit. And let us work toward complete holiness because we fear God.' (2 Cor. 7:1)

- **Truth is NOT relative;** By nature, truth must remain constant and cannot change based on an individual's perspective. The promotion of relativity of truth is claimed to be for the purpose of peace and tolerance, but in actuality it encourages the compromise of beliefs. As Christians we are to be considerate of others, but we must not deny our faith for the sake of 'peace and tolerance'! We deny that Jesus is the ONLY way when we accept that truth is relative. (John 14:6)

We must remember that 'this is a trustworthy saying: If we die with Him, we will also live with Him. If we endure hardship, we will reign with Him. If we deny Him, He will deny us.' (2 Tim. 2:11-12).

God has revealed Himself to us, and His revelation is trustworthy: 'This God—His way is perfect; the word of the LORD proves true; He is a shield for all those who take refuge in Him.' (Ps. 18:30, ESV).

This might cause debate until the end of the world, but we must remember not to get caught up in pointless arguments. Ultimately, 'truthful words stand the test of time, but lies are soon exposed' (Prov. 12:19), and exposed they will be, be it by God's mercy in the illumination that is salvation, or by Christ Jesus' glorious return!

- **<u>Hello Compassion, Goodbye Apathy</u>;** It might seem strange to some, but it is surprisingly easy to be apathetic (even after coming to Christ). The only difference in this being to what degree it happens.

Sure, we can frown at some things and be happy about some things, but tell me; what would deeply impact us, and yet we wouldn't see cause to make petition before God regarding it? Whose sorrow would deeply grieve our being that we wouldn't rend our broken hearts to God, pleading for His comfort and healing? What good news would raise our spirits so, that we wouldn't offer a prayer of praise and adoration, thanking God for such mercies?
We might understand some people's plights, but we rarely truly open our hearts. If we had compassion like we ought, I believe the Church would be so much more effective and relevant!

Paul exhorts the Body to 'rejoice with those who rejoice, weep with those who weep.' (Rom. 12:15, ESV).
We must learn to open our hearts to feel, our hands to give, our feet to evangelize, our shoulders to bear burdens,

our time to encourage, our minds to counsel, our mouths to advise, and our spirits to prayer.

- Be anxious about nothing, pray about everything;

Prayer is a key part of a believer's life. We are exhorted to never stop praying (1 Thess. 5:17, Col. 4:2). In the normal course of life, we find many reasons to stress and worry and fret. This is true for all, believer or not.

C.S. Lewis writes this message in his book 'Mere Christianity':

"All your wishes and hopes for the day rush at you like wild animals. And the first job each morning consists simply in shoving them all back; in listening to that other voice, taking that other point of view, letting that other larger, stronger, quieter life come flowing in.
What we have been told is how we men can be drawn into Christ—can become part of that wonderful present which the young Prince of the universe wants to offer to His Father—that present which is Himself and therefore us in Him. It is the only thing we were made for. And there are strange, exciting hints in the Bible that when we are drawn in, a great many other things in Nature will begin to come right, The bad dream will be over: it will be morning."

We must not neglect spending time with our Lord each morning. Let's follow David's example: 'Listen to my cry for help, my King and my God, for I pray to no one but You. Listen to my voice in the morning, LORD. Each morning I bring my requests to You and wait expectantly.' (Ps. 5:2-3)

The Church in Philippi were encouraged: 'Don't worry about anything; instead, pray about everything. Tell God what you need, and thank Him for all He has done. Then you will experience God's peace, which exceeds anything we can understand. His peace will guard your hearts and minds as you live in Christ Jesus.' (Phil. 4:6-7)

- Seeking wisdom is the wisest thing you can do; If the fear of the LORD is the foundation of wisdom and true knowledge (Prov. 1:7, 9:10), then it stands to reason that if you fear the LORD, you would 'tune your ears to wisdom, and concentrate on understanding. Cry out for insight, and ask for understanding. Search for them as you would for silver; seek them like hidden treasures.' (Prov. 2:2-4)

Solomon says, 'Getting wisdom is the wisest thing you can do! And whatever else you do, develop good judgment.' (Prov. 4:7)

Gone is the time of ignorance when we might have been excused (with some rebuke and loving discipline) for our lack of sense, but as we grow up we are required to put aside our folly in quest for wisdom, which the LORD grants freely to all who ask (Prov. 2:6, James 1:5-8, 1 Kings 3:5-12).

Only with wisdom do we gain discernment and receive understanding about the issues of life. For 'the wisdom of the prudent is to give thought to their ways, but the folly of fools is deception.' (Prov. 14:8, NIV)

And what way does God grant us wisdom? Through His Word (Ps. 19:7b, Ps. 119:105), and the counsel of the wise (Prov. 13:20, Col. 3:16), to name but a few.

- **Escape the snare of unproductive comparison;** It is understandable to look to people you admire or who operate in a similar fashion as you, but beware! This is an easy invitation for envy to come in and lay hold of your heart. It's not long before encouragement and motivation become resentment and depression, and you soon forget that your worth is not in how well you do something better than someone else.

As a believer, your identity is NOT in your achievements or adeptness at something, but rather, your identity is in Christ (Col. 3:3, Gal. 2:20, Col. 3:10-11, Eph. 2:19-21). Before we begin to question why we do not have what others have and make them idols, we must sober up to the warnings of the apostles:

'Dear friends, I warn you as "temporary residents and foreigners" to keep away from worldly desires that wage war against your very souls.' **(1 Pet. 2:11)**

'Dear children, keep away from anything that might take God's place in your hearts.' **(1 John 5:21)**

Be encouraged, and keep your sights on Christ as you follow Him into the new year, where He already awaits us!

A Short Meditation on Proverbs 18:21

Prov. 18:21

- 'The tongue can bring death or life; those who love to talk will reap the consequences.' (NLT)

- 'Death and life are in the power of the tongue, and those who love it will eat its fruit.' (NKJV)

- 'The tongue has the power of life and death, and those who love it will eat its fruit.' (NIV)

This is a proverb that has been grossly misquoted; this proverb talks about the effects and consequences of our speech, not some ability to make a person fall dead, or to 'speak' life into people.

(I suppose metaphorically we could debate this, since sharing the gospel by which one can be saved is as the aroma of life/death to those who receive/deny it <2 Cor. 2:14-17>, but the times I've heard this misquoted, I don't believe they were speaking metaphorically.)

We must not take passages of Scripture and twist them to make us think more highly of ourselves than we ought.

A simple example I could use to portray the meaning of this Scripture is that, as was decreed by law, a person was condemned/acquitted based on the testimony of two or more witnesses (Deut. 17:2-6, Deut. 19:15), and so one of the commandments passed was that '"You must not testify falsely against your neighbor' (Ex. 20:16), as a false witness could lead to the death of an innocent person.

One of the main themes of this book of wisdom is that speech should be carefully and prudently minded, and this verse reminds us why: for death and life are in the power of the tongue, and your words can bring healing or destruction to yourself and those around you.

Prov. 10:19 - 'Too much talk leads to sin. Be sensible and keep your mouth shut.'

Prov. 12:6 - 'The words of the wicked are like a murderous ambush, but the words of the godly save lives.'

Prov. 13:3 - 'Those who control their tongue will have a long life; opening your mouth can ruin everything.'

Ps. 34:12-13 - 'Does anyone want to live a life that is long and prosperous? Then keep your tongue from speaking evil and your lips from telling lies!'

Matt. 12:35-37 - 'A good person produces good things from the treasury of a good heart, and an evil person produces evil things from the treasury of an evil heart. And I tell you this, you must give an account on judgment day for every idle word you speak. The words you say will either acquit you or condemn you.'

Commenting on Proverbs 18:21, John Gill writes,

"Death and life are in the power of the tongue... Of witnesses, according to the testimony they bear; of judges, according to the sentence they pass; of teachers, according to the doctrine they preach; of all men, who, by their well or ill speaking, bring death or life to themselves and others. Some, by their tongues, by the too free use of them, or falsehood they utter, are the cause of death to themselves and others; and some, by their silence, or by their prudent speech and prevalent intercession, secure or obtain life for themselves and others; yea, judgment at the last day will proceed according to a man's words, "By thy words thou shalt be justified, and by thy words thou shalt be condemned", Matthew 12:37; the tongue is the instrument either of a great deal of good, or of a great deal of evil;

and they that love it shall eat the fruit thereof; that delight to be talkative; that love to use the tongue, whether in a good or in a bad way, shall accordingly be recompensed; shall enjoy the advantages or disadvantages arising from it."

(See also James 3:1-12)

I pray this meditation has been encouraging ^_^

The Cost of Carrying Your Cross: A Short Meditation

Jesus our Lord said, "'If you want to be My disciple, you must hate everyone else by comparison—your father and mother, wife and children, brothers and sisters-yes, even your own life. Otherwise, you cannot be My disciple. And if you do not carry your own cross and follow Me, you cannot be My disciple.

"But don't begin until you count the cost. For who would begin construction of a building without first calculating the cost to see if there is enough money to finish it? Otherwise, you might complete only the foundation before running out of money, and then everyone would laugh at you. They would say, 'There's the person who started that building and couldn't afford to finish it!'

"Or what king would go to war against another king without first sitting down with his counselors to discuss whether his army of 10,000 could defeat the 20,000 soldiers marching against him? And if he can't, he will send a delegation to discuss terms of peace while the enemy is still far away.

So you cannot become My disciple without giving up everything you own.' **(Luke 14:26-33)**

Paul said, '...I once thought these things were valuable, but now I consider them worthless because of what Christ has done. Yes, everything else is worthless when compared with the infinite value of knowing Christ Jesus my Lord. For His sake I have discarded everything else, counting it all as garbage, so that I could gain Christ and become one with Him.' **(Phil. 3:7-9a)**

And He also said, '...But if we are to share His glory, we must also share His suffering.' **(Rom. 8:17b)**

And Peter mentioned, 'Dear friends, don't be surprised at the fiery trials you are going through, as if something strange were happening to you. Instead, be very glad—for these trials make you partners with Christ in His suffering, so that you will have the wonderful joy of seeing His glory when it is revealed to all the world.' **(1 Pet. 4:12-13)**

Be not deceived brethren; the cost of following Christ is high—it is your very lives. But the reward of following Christ is eternal—it is your very souls! Count nothing more important than knowing Christ and being numbered among His saints!

That lovely hymn goes:

"Knowing You, Jesus, knowing You,
There is no greater thing;
You're my all, You're the best,
You're my joy, my righteousness,
And I love You Lord!" (Graham Kendrick, 'Knowing You')

With an eternal perspective in view (Col. 3:1-4), surely we see how vain everything else is, and how it all pales in comparison.

Solomon writes:

'History merely repeats itself. It has all been done before. Nothing under the sun is truly new. Sometimes some people say, "Here is something new!" But actually it is old; nothing is ever truly new.' (Ecc. 1:9-10)

John warns us not to love the world and its ways (1 John 2:15-17), and Paul exhorts us to renew our minds and not be conformed to the ways of the world (Rom. 12:2). It is easy to be sidetracked by the world in this Incredible Walk we're on, so we must remember to stay alert against all the scheming of our enemy to divert our attention.

Indeed, we must stay focused at ALL times. Daunting and tasking as it is, we must remember God's promises of renewed strength and unrelenting mercy:

Isa. 40:29-31 - 'He gives power to the weak and strength to the powerless. Even youths will become weak and tired, and young men will fall in exhaustion. But those who trust in the LORD will find new strength. They will soar high on wings like eagles. They will run and not grow weary. They will walk and not faint.'

Heb. 4:15-16 - 'This High Priest of ours understands our weaknesses, for He faced all of the same testings we do, yet He did not sin.
So let us come boldly to the throne of our gracious God. There we will receive His mercy, and we will find grace to help us when we need it most.'

2 Cor. 12:10 - '...That's why I take pleasure in my weaknesses, and in the insults, hardships, persecutions, and troubles that I suffer for Christ. For when I am weak, then I am strong.'

Now this means more than being alert about spiritual matters. Indeed, it permeates throughout our whole lives.

Jesus isn't only Lord over our churchly activities, nor is He only Lord over our prayer lives; He is Lord over everything we do, and we must remember that from the moment of conversion when we surrendered our lives to be slaves of Christ, we pledged our allegiance:

'My old self has been crucified with Christ. It is no longer I who live, but Christ lives in me. So I live in this earthly body by trusting in the Son of God, who loved me and gave Himself for me.' (Gal. 2:20)

Our everyday lives and actions must reflect this. We live to please Him in all things (1 Cor. 10:31). This is especially true of what we open our minds up to, like entertainment for example. We must not only resist what is inherently sinful, but we must also wage war against anything that would either cause us to scoff at what God takes pleasure in, or laugh at what God hates. Do not open yourselves to subconsciously ridiculing God and His ways for the sake of your entertainment. We must remember that God is GOD first, before He is our Father. He loves us with all the passion and grace of Heaven, but He loves His glory more and WILL uphold His standards:

Hab. 1:13a - '...But You [God] are pure and cannot stand the sight of evil. Will You wink at their treachery?'

Prov. 14:2 - 'Those who follow the right path fear the LORD; those who take the wrong path despise Him.'

Prov. 15:10a - 'Whoever abandons the right path will be severely disciplined...'

Our old lives are dead and buried, and our new lives are lived under the authority and rule of Christ Jesus our Lord. All who have made the choice to enter into this beautiful covenant must count the cost so they are not surprised by the absence of a cotton-candy, fluffy, prosperous life. (Food for Thought: If our Master died hanging on a cross, why on earth would we expect to sleep on a bed of money?)

In addition to this, they also must keep their eyes on the Kingdom, and on the One who is worthy of all praise, reverence, worship, and adoration, now and forevermore! Amen!

And so, I would like to encourage you by closing with these passages, and I hope you're blessed by them:

'Think back on those early days when you first learned about Christ. Remember how you remained faithful even though it meant terrible suffering. Sometimes you were exposed to public ridicule and were beaten, and sometimes you helped others who were suffering the same things.

You suffered along with those who were thrown into jail, and when all you owned was taken from you, you accepted it with joy. You knew there were better things waiting for you that will last forever.

So do not throw away this confident trust in the Lord. Remember the great reward it brings you! Patient endurance is what you need now, so that you will continue to do God's will. Then you will receive all that He has promised.

"For in just a little while, the Coming One will come and not delay. And My righteous ones will live by faith. But I will take no pleasure in anyone who turns away."

But we are not like those who turn away from God to their own destruction. We are the faithful ones, whose souls will be saved.' **(Heb. 10:32-39)**

'So if you are suffering in a manner that pleases God, keep doing what is right, and trust your lives to the God who created you, for He will never fail you.' **(1 Pet. 4:19)**

Self-Examination: A Short Meditation

"What I would give to walk in the Light... but what I hide has made me lame..." (Bethany Dillon, 'Get Up and Walk')

Lately I find my heart increasingly burdened. Not because I'm doing anything exceptionally bad, but sometimes I get the feeling that my Walk isn't quite where it should be (I know we all get that feeling). So digging a little deeper, I realized that perhaps I still have some sin I'm clinging to that is holding me back from coming before Christ wholeheartedly. Could it be that there was a part of my old life—a part of my old nature—that I wasn't letting go of?

The thought made me feel lukewarm, like I was on the fence. Sure I had confessed and professed Jesus as my Lord and Savior, but He has made it quite clear:

'If you love Me, obey My commandments.' (John 14:15)

'...And we can be sure that we know Him if we obey His commandments. If someone claims, "I know God," but doesn't obey God's commandments, that person is a liar and is not living in the truth. But those who obey God's word truly show how completely they love Him. That is how we know we are living in Him.' (1 John 2:3-5)

If I saddle the fence in certain areas of my life, and cling on to sinful behavior and habits as opposed to striving for righteousness in ALL things, how can I honestly say I am His disciple? How can I call Him 'Lord', and not give Him every aspect of my being?

1 John 2:6 - 'Those who say they live in God should live their lives as Jesus did.'

Luke 6:46 - '"Why do you call Me, 'Lord, Lord,' and do not do what I say?' (NIV)

Reading on from the last verse, Jesus illustrates how those who LISTEN to His words AND practice them are founded on solid ground, but the ones who remain hearers alone will not withstand the torrents of life:

Prov. 10:25 - 'When the storms of life come, the wicked are whirled away, but the godly have a lasting foundation.'

We must examine ourselves DAILY, working out our salvation with FEAR and TREMBLING, not in a laid-back, 'all is well' attitude.

Prov. 16:2 - 'People may be pure in their own eyes, but the LORD examines their motives.'

2 Pet. 1:10 - '...So, dear brothers and sisters, work hard to prove that you really are among those God has called and chosen. Do these things, and you will never fall away.'

If we let sin persist in our lives, it hinders our walk (John 3:20-21), but if we trust and have faith in Jesus Christ and the power of His atonement, we walk in freedom (1 John 1:8-10). Don't let your sins keep you groping around in the darkness. Confess and repent, and turn to Him for grace and forgiveness, that you might walk in life; good intentions aren't enough to get you into the Kingdom of God (John 3:3, Matt. 7:21-23).

'...Because we have these promises, dear friends, let us cleanse ourselves from everything that can defile our body or spirit. And let us work toward complete holiness because we fear God.' **(2 Cor. 7:1)**

Be encouraged.

Habits & Motivation: A Short Meditation, Part 1

Grace and peace to you all, and I pray this meets you in good health, or at least, meets you in a place of better reliance on God since I last wrote to you.

First off, I'd like to perish any thought or assumption that this message comes from a place of pride; to be honest, the amount of times I've done the wrong thing—or failed to do the right thing, which coincidentally is the same as doing the wrong thing—vastly outweigh the amount of times I've done the right thing... Since I've been a Christian.

It's not all lost though! That statement comes with an underlying testimony. The fact that I've done the right thing even ONCE (or indeed sought to do the right thing) is a testament to God's grace and work in my life, as none can please God in our flesh, and so it shows that I am being transformed! HalleluYah! (Rom. 8:5-8, Phil. 1:6, 2 Cor. 5:17)

Okay, so with the introductions out of the way, let's get to the topic at hand. We'll start with motivation ^_^.

Feel free to disagree with me (I'm only human), but I believe that anything done without an underlying motive or motivation is nothing but a meaningless chore done in vain; a waste of time and energy.
If you do something without a reason, then it probably lacks a desired outcome or a desire for proper action. After all, if you have no reason to do something, why would you care how you do it or what the end result is?

So then, if we go by the assumption that anything worthwhile we do in our lives is fuelled by an underlying motive, then I'd say that what our motives are is a topic of pretty darn importance, wouldn't you?

Now, I'd like to avoid the philosophical and morally-challenging debate of ends and means (i.e. if what you achieve is justified by the methods you use), and so I will assume, reader, that you do not partake in the thought of 'using evil to conquer evil' (Rom. 12:17-21).

I am more interested in answering the question, "what do I live for?" And if I'm quick to say, "I live to serve God, obviously," (as that is what I think my Christian friends want to hear), then I'd ask myself, "why? What's in it for me?"

We'll start with **"what do I live for?"**

It doesn't take a genius to realize that nothing on this earth is permanent. Think again if you think you're the most ambitious person to walk this earth; people have been striving for fame and fortune before your great-great-great-greater-greatest-grandparents were even conceived! The wisest man (apart from Christ), who also happened to be the wealthiest man (no surprise there) to walk the earth had this to say:

'Everything is wearisome beyond description. No matter how much we see, we are never satisfied. No matter how much we hear, we are not content. History merely repeats itself. It has all been done before.
Nothing under the sun is truly new. Sometimes people say, "Here is something new!" But actually it is old;

nothing is ever truly new.
We don't remember what happened in the past, and in future generations, no one will remember what we are doing now...
...I observed everything going on under the sun, and really, it is all meaningless—like chasing the wind.' (Ecc. 1:8-11, v14)

Even if you don't believe what the Bible has to say, at least you would notice the truth of that statement in the world around you (unless you've intentionally chosen to ignore it).

I spoke to a corner store owner the other day. He stood there with a big wad of money and a grim expression. "I'm caught up in the rat race," he said. "So much bills to pay. Even after that, there's more problems."
I don't think he's read the Bible, but even he had an idea about the truth of the way the world works.
You make money to spend money, and you spend money to make money. You work hard to please people so they make you famous, and then the same people who make you famous turn on you and your fame goes down the drain.

If your motive for living is to go around in circles like that then... Look forward to spending life living like a dog chasing its own tail!

Don't get me wrong, there's nothing wrong with trying to make money, as you cannot really survive in this modern civilization without getting involved with money, but money is nowhere near valuable enough to dedicate your life to it (Matt. 6:24-25, 1 Tim. 6:6-10).

Those who say they're living for God; first I commend you! At least you're looking beyond this temporary space to what is eternal.

Let's then ask the next question: **"Why? What's in it for me?"**

- If the answer to this goes back to money (disclaimer: prosperity preachers' fans might want to stop reading here), then I'm afraid you've started on the path only to make a U-turn:

'...These people always cause trouble. Their minds are corrupt, and they have turned their backs on the truth.

To them, a show of godliness is just a way to become wealthy. Yet true godliness with contentment is itself great wealth. After all, we brought nothing with us when we came into the world, and we can't take anything with us when we leave it.

So if we have enough food and clothing, let us be content.' (1 Tim. 6:5-8)

- If the answer is to live a 'peaceful' life then I'm afraid that's a hit-and-miss too:

'...So then, since Christ suffered physical pain, you must arm yourselves with the same attitude He had, and be ready to suffer, too. For if you have suffered physically for Christ, you have finished with sin. You won't spend the rest of your lives chasing your own desires, but you will be anxious to do the will of God.' (1 Pet. 4:1-2)

- If you think living for God will make you liked or famous then I think someone might have sold you a dream:

'"If the world hates you, remember that it hated Me first. The world would love you as one of its own if you belonged to it, but you are no longer part of the world. I chose you to come out of the world, so it hates you. Do you remember what I told you? 'A slave is not greater than the master.' Since they persecuted Me, naturally they will persecute you. And if they had listened to Me, they would listen to you. They will do all this to you because of Me, for they have rejected the One who sent Me.' (John 15:18-21)

'...I have given them Your word. And the world hates them because they do not belong to the world, just as I do not belong to the world.' (John 17:14)

'...Of course, your former friends are surprised when you no longer plunge into the flood of wild and destructive things they do. So they slander you.' (1 Pet. 4:4)

So that this message does not become too long, I'll just quickly wrap up with this:

Ps. 73:24-26 - 'You guide Me with your counsel, leading me to a glorious destiny.
Whom have I in heaven but You? I desire You more than anything on earth.
My health may fail, and my spirit may grow weak, but God remains the strength of my heart; He is mine

forever.'

Some things this passage points out for us:

- 'You guide me with Your counsel' - A life directed by God is what we ought to seek (Ps. 119:105).

- '...leading me to a glorious destiny' - God has A LOT more intended for us than our feeble minds can think or comprehend (Eph. 2:10, Eph. 3:20-21).

- 'Whom have I in heaven but You?' - God is all that matters. It is not about Heaven, the place with mansions and no more pain or weeping; but it is about being in eternal fellowship with our God and Creator (John 17:3, 1 John 3:1-3).

- 'I desire You more than anything on earth' - God is worth more than life itself, and so He ought to be our greatest desire, and hence our primary motivation in all things (1 John 2:15-17, Col. 3:23, 1 Cor. 10:31, 1 John 5:21).

- 'My health may fail, and my spirit may grow weak, but

God remains the strength of my heart...' - Even in our weaknesses, He is our source of strength (Ps. 121:1-3, Isa. 40:28-31, Gal. 2:20).

- 'He is mine forever' - The Eternal One has promised Himself to us through His son Jesus Christ (Lam. 3:21-25, Rom. 8:38-39, Rev. 22:3-5).

Such a wealth of truth! And that was only three verses of the Bible! So much more can be said about these things, but I hope that our brief look on the topic encouraged you, and will *motivate* you to find out more for yourself ^_^

So... I think this message is quite long enough as it is, and unfortunately I won't be able to get on to the second topic of habits. Maybe some other time perhaps?

Have a blessed day!

Habits & Motivation: A Short Meditation, Part 2

I finally got around to finishing this meditation. Since we were able to briefly cover motivation in the first part, let's move on to habits.

When I think of habits, one of the main things that come to mind is the need for renewal of the mind:

'Don't copy the behavior and customs of this world, but let God transform you into a new person by changing the way you think. Then you will learn to know God's will for you, which is good and pleasing and perfect.' **(Rom. 12:2)**

Why? Because we all, for the most part, have been brainwashed! From our birth we inherited a fallen nature:

Job 25:4 - 'How can a mortal be innocent before God? Can anyone born of a woman be pure?'

Ps. 51:5 - '...For I was born a sinner—yes, from the moment my mother conceived me.'

Rom. 5:12 - 'When Adam sinned, sin entered the world.

Adam's sin brought death, so death spread to everyone, for everyone sinned.'

And since then, living in this fallen world, we have picked up (knowingly or unknowingly) the customs, morals, and ways of thinking all around us that are contrary to God:

Eph. 2:1-3 - 'Once you were dead because of your disobedience and your many sins. You used to live in sin, just like the rest of the world, obeying the devil—the commander of the powers in the unseen world. He is the spirit at work in the hearts of those who refuse to obey God.
All of us used to live that way, following the passionate desires and inclinations of our sinful nature. By our very nature we were subject to God's anger, just like everyone else.'

Gal. 5:19-21 - 'When you follow the desires of your sinful nature, the results are very clear: sexual immorality, impurity, lustful pleasures, idolatry, sorcery, hostility, quarreling, jealousy, outbursts of anger, selfish ambition, dissension, division, envy, drunkenness, wild parties, and other sins like these. Let me tell you again, as I have before, that anyone living that sort of life will not inherit the Kingdom of God.'

So then, when you add to our inherent sinfulness a lifetime of living contrary to the ways of God, how hard it must be to change that!
However, at just the right time, hope appeared:

Isa. 9:2 - 'The people who walk in darkness will see a great light. For those who live in a land of deep darkness, a light will shine.'

John 1:5 - 'The light shines in the darkness, and the darkness can never extinguish it.'

Rom. 5:6 - 'When we were utterly helpless, Christ came at just the right time and died for us sinners.'

Col. 1:13-14 - '...For He has rescued us from the kingdom of darkness and transferred us into the Kingdom of His dear Son, who purchased our freedom and forgave our sins.'

2 Cor. 5:21 - '...For God made Christ, who never sinned, to be the offering for our sin, so that we could be made right with God through Christ.'

What amazing truth! In our helplessness, Christ died for us, freeing us from our slavery to sin (Rom. 6:17-18) and making us anew (2 Cor. 5:17) after we had all gone astray (Ecc. 7:29).

I speak of the gospel as a prelude to this message because we CANNOT change ourselves by ourselves:

Rom. 7:14-20 - '...So the trouble is not with the law, for it is spiritual and good. The trouble is with me, for I am all too human, a slave to sin. I don't really understand myself, for I want to do what is right, but I don't do it. Instead, I do what I hate. But if I know that what I am doing is wrong, this shows that I agree that the law is good.
So I am not the one doing wrong; it is sin living in me that does it. And I know that nothing good lives in me, that is, in my sinful nature. I want to do what is right, but I can't. I want to do what is good, but I don't. I don't want to do what is wrong, but I do it anyway. But if I do what I don't want to do, I am not really the one doing wrong; it is sin living in me that does it.'

Some might find my statement extreme. After all, people

DO change over time right? Some people drop bad practices, and some pick up good ones. Isn't it a bit too "religious" to claim that one cannot be changed except by being a Christian?

Well, I suppose my statement was made on an assumption that goes back to our first topic of motivation. What is the motive for wanting to change in the first place? Your family? Your peers? Wanting to look good?

As for those who choose to live a life motivated by serving God, then seeking change for reasons such as trying to live morally right isn't enough. It isn't enough to just ACT a certain way:

Rom. 8:6-8 - '...letting your sinful nature control your mind leads to death. But letting the Spirit control your mind leads to life and peace. For the sinful nature is always hostile to God. It never did obey God's laws, and it never will.
That's why those who are still under the control of their sinful nature can never please God.'

Here is where the gospel comes in, because those who try to 'change' and please God by themselves can never do so:

'As the Scriptures say,

"No one is righteous—not even one. No one is truly wise; no one is seeking God. All have turned away; all have become useless. No one does good, not a single one."
"Their talk is foul, like the stench from an open grave. Their tongues are filled with lies."
"Snake venom drips from their lips."
"Their mouths are full of cursing and bitterness."
"They rush to commit murder. Destruction and misery always follow them. They don't know where to find peace."
"They have no fear of God at all."' **(Rom. 3:10-18)**

ONLY the work of Christ can save you; nothing we do can work up the kind of right living that God requires:

'God saved you by His grace when you believed. And you can't take credit for this; it is a gift from God. Salvation is not a reward for the good things we have done, so none of us can boast about it.' **(Eph. 2:8-9)**

So then, now that we have been saved (by the work of Christ, not ours), we are now free to actually do the right things that please God (Rom. 6:6-14).

We can now move on from the introduction to the topic of habits!

Scripture consistently tells us to 'put off' our 'old nature' and 'put on' our 'new nature', while never failing to remind us that it is the work of the Spirit within us that makes this all possible (see Rom. 8:12-13, Gal. 5:16, Eph. 4:22-23, Phil. 2:12-13, Col. 3:10).

I will not assume to have some sort of equation or formula for righteous living... Well, except this:

'How can a young person stay pure? By obeying Your word... I have hidden Your word in my heart, that I might not sin against You.' (Ps. 119:9, v11)

The word of God is 'a lamp to guide my feet and a light for my path' (Ps. 119:105), and it leads all His children in the right path, helped along by the Spirit in understanding and discernment.

So, getting to the core of this message, there are three things (I can remember at the moment) I've noticed, and I thought to share them:

1) The Word of God is more specific about righteous living than some might think:

Often times people talk about how the Bible isn't clear on certain things, and you just have to rely on the convictions you feel to decide whether or not you are on the right track. However, some things are made clear:

1 Pet. 1:13-16 - '...So think clearly and exercise self-control. Look forward to the gracious salvation that will come to you when Jesus Christ is revealed to the world. So you must live as God's obedient children. Don't slip back into your old ways of living to satisfy your own desires. You didn't know any better then. But now you must be holy in everything you do, just as God who chose you is holy.
For the Scriptures say, "You must be holy because I am holy."'

Now, granted that the Bible does not cover ALL possible situations (although these can be addressed by proper application of the intent of Scripture), it does cover common issues such as laughing at other people's expense, sexual immorality, swearing/bad language, anger, gossip, laziness, pride, idleness, slander, greed, selfishness, drunkenness, and the list goes on! (See Col. 3, Gal. 5:16-26, Eph. 4:17-32, Eph. 5:1-12).

Identifying what habits we possess that are contrary to what God desires in us is a good place to start.

I pray we can all find this as a truth in our lives:

'You have had enough in the past of the evil things that godless people enjoy-their immorality and lust, their feasting and drunkenness and wild parties, and their terrible worship of idols.
Of course, your former friends are surprised when you no longer plunge into the flood of wild and destructive things they do. So they slander you. But remember that they will have to face God, who will judge everyone, both the living and the dead.' **(1 Pet. 4:3-5)**

2) Who you hang around with has more of an effect than some might think:

"Bad company corrupts good character" (1 Cor. 15:33)

indeed! When you hang around people long enough, you start to talk, act, and think like them. Influencing one another is a basic truth in friendships, but the danger is who is having the greater influence?

'Walk with the wise and become wise; associate with fools and get in trouble.' - **Prov. 13:20**

'Don't befriend angry people or associate with hot-tempered people, or you will learn to be like them and endanger your soul.' - **Prov. 22:24-25**

'Run from anything that stimulates youthful lusts. Instead, pursue righteous living, faithfulness, love, and peace. Enjoy the companionship of those who call on the Lord with pure hearts.' - **2 Tim. 2:22**

I'm not saying that we should only have Christian friends, because contrary to most of our desires, we cannot live in a bubble. However, it might be wise to identify those who are having a negative effect on you and that you probably should stay away from (or maybe not be as close to), and those who you have the opportunity to influence for the good.

3) Sometimes you have to 'force' it:

A while ago, I came across Psalm 5:1-3:

'O LORD, hear me as I pray; pay attention to my groaning. Listen to my cry for help, my King and my God, for I pray to no one but You. Listen to my voice in the morning, LORD. Each morning I bring my requests to You and wait expectantly.'

After reading this, I longed for such a relationship; to begin my day with the LORD. Not that I didn't pray or read the Word when I got up before, but it didn't seem enough (or right) that my time with Him in the morning should be dependent upon what time I got up that day; it had to be constant (to the best of my ability). So, I chose a time which wasn't too unrealistic to meet, yet wasn't too comfortable that I wouldn't be diligent about.

Now, I thought it would be easy. I thought since I wanted a better relationship with God, He would snap His fingers or something, and I would have no issue waking up early, praying and dwelling in the Word.

To this day, it's a battle every morning to do this—and I do fail sometimes, but His grace is ever-present and He sustains me in this decision I have made (Prov. 16:3).

That is a simple and straightforward example to what I mean. I can't speak for most, but I always used to assume that a godly decision would be an easy decision. Since it's for God, surely He would make it easy, right?

Ha!

After reflecting on the narrative of Scripture, I had to 'renew my mind' about that one!

'We can rejoice, too, when we run into problems and trials, for we know that they help us develop endurance. And endurance develops strength of character, and character strengthens our confident hope of salvation. And this hope will not lead to disappointment. For we know how dearly God loves us, because He has given us the Holy Spirit to fill our hearts with His love.' (Rom. 5:3-5)

Making a choice to better serve God is a product of His

work within us (Phil. 2:13), but it doesn't relieve us of the work we have to do (Phil. 2:12). If anything, it is even harder because we are going against what our flesh wants, and waging war against ourselves each time:

'The sinful nature wants to do evil, which is just the opposite of what the Spirit wants. And the Spirit gives us desires that are the opposite of what the sinful nature desires. These two forces are constantly fighting each other, so you are not free to carry out your good intentions.' (Gal. 5:17)

The next issue I came across within this was that if I had to FORCE myself to do it, then didn't that mean it wasn't the right choice? Shouldn't the right choices just 'flow' and 'be natural'?

Again, I had to examine my way of thinking about that!

'...So, dear brothers and sisters, work hard to prove that you really are among those God has called and chosen. Do these things, and you will never fall away.' (2 Pet. 1:10)

If 'no one is seeking after God' (Rom. 3:11), and the 'spirit is willing but the flesh is weak' (Matt. 26:41), then what is 'natural' about us wanting to please God?

'...For the sinful nature is always hostile to God. It never did obey God's laws, and it never will. That's why those who are still under the control of their sinful nature can never please God.' (Rom. 8:7-8)

It is an act of God's grace and intervention that we even desire to please Him! If we are called to wage war against our sin each day, then it shouldn't be a surprise that the decision to serve God instead of pleasing our flesh doesn't come easy! However, we do not have to do it alone; His Spirit helps us in our weaknesses and He is faithful to keep us! (2 Tim. 2:13)

Countless times I've found myself having to force myself to do something (even though for the most part of me, I'd rather not), not to be moralistic, but because I knew it was the right thing to do (as revealed in His Word) and it pleased God. Eventually, what I started begrudgingly turned into a habit, which turned into a character trait, and soon before long, I could see the blessings in the fruit it produced!

Wow, my meditations are getting longer :/... Anyway, to summarize:

- Identify your motive for wanting to pick up or drop a habit

- Identify and examine the habits you have already with the Word of God to see if they are pleasing to God

- Take note of who you hang around with; bad company corrupts good character

- Realize that you cannot change on your own; only through the Spirit can we be transformed and please God

- Just because you choose to serve God better doesn't mean it will be easy!
Yeah I'll stop there. I congratulate anyone who read this far! I pray it has been enlightening, or encouraging, or a good read at least?

Have a blessed day! ^_^

Who Is Good?: A Short Meditation

Ps. 119:68 - 'You are good and do only good; teach me Your decrees.'

Unlike us, God isn't bound by a moral code or law; He is inherently good. This means that He doesn't do things because they are good, but rather, whatever He does is good BECAUSE He does it. He is the standard for goodness, and an example of this is shown in Proverbs 16:11 - 'The LORD demands accurate scales and balances; He sets the standards for fairness.'

Jesus pointed this out when He was asked a question:

'Once a religious leader asked Jesus this question: "Good Teacher, what should I do to inherit eternal life?" "Why do you call Me good?" Jesus asked him. "Only God is truly good.' (Luke 18:18-19)

We, on the other hand, naturally do the WRONG things (Rom. 3:10-13), and so we must never assume to be in the right. Even if we do or act better than our peers or friends, it doesn't make us good, it just makes us appear less wicked than THEY are. We end up making THEM the standard of what is right and wrong, and then judge ourselves based on that. But the Word of God teaches us that we shouldn't use ourselves as a standard:

2 Cor. 10:12 - '...Oh, don't worry; we wouldn't dare say that we are as wonderful as these other men who tell you how important they are! But they are only comparing themselves with each other, using themselves as the standard of measurement. How ignorant!'

This makes sense; after all, how can we trust ourselves to be the standard for good? The morals of our society are constantly changing, and what would have been unspeakable before is now a norm. The funny thing is, humankind has been going through this same cycle of bad is good and good is bad long before we got here. And so, if we are to have a standard by which we examine ourselves, it must be a standard which never changes, and can be relied on...

Ps. 119:68 says, 'You are good and do only good...', and

Hebrews 13:8 says that 'Jesus Christ is the same yesterday, today, and forever'. With this we know that God is never-changing, and is also the standard for good, because all He does IS good!

So, we know God is good, and He is the standard. So how do we examine ourselves with His standard? By using His Word:

Ps. 19:7 - 'The law of the Lord is perfect, reviving the soul; the testimony of the Lord is sure, making wise the simple.' (ESV)

Ps. 119:105 - 'Your word is a lamp to my feet and a light to my path.'

So, now we have the standard by which we can examine ourselves, but there lies another problem. According to the standard, we FAIL the examination:

Rom. 3:23 - '...For everyone has sinned; we all fall short of God's glorious standard.'

Oh dear! We're all doomed!

...Or are we?

Rom. 3:21-22 - '...But now God has shown us a way to be made right with Him without keeping the requirements of the law, as was promised in the writings of Moses and the prophets long ago. We are made right with God by placing our faith in Jesus Christ. And this is true for everyone who believes, no matter who we are.'

Thank God! Because of what Jesus Christ has done, God's standard is met in (and only in) Him! But this doesn't mean we can disregard the instructions in the Word of God:

Rom. 3:31 - 'Well then, if we emphasize faith, does this mean that we can forget about the law? Of course not! In fact, only when we have faith do we truly fulfill the law.'

So then, we have been freed by the work of Jesus so that we can actually do the right thing now:

Rom. 6:14-15, v18 - 'Sin is no longer your master, for you no longer live under the requirements of the law. Instead, you live under the freedom of God's grace.

Well then, since God's grace has set us free from the law, does that mean we can go on sinning? Of course not!...
...Now you are free from your slavery to sin, and you have become slaves to righteous living.'

We do this by reading, meditating, and putting into action the Word of God daily:

Ps. 119:9, v11 - 'How can a young person stay pure? By obeying Your word...
I have hidden Your word in my heart, that I might not sin against You.'

Rom. 12:2 - 'Don't copy the behavior and customs of this world, but let God transform you into a new person by changing the way you think. Then you will learn to know God's will for you, which is good and pleasing and perfect.'

...And also by letting the Holy Spirit work in and lead us in all things:

Eph. 4:21-23 - 'Since you have heard about Jesus and have learned the truth that comes from Him, throw off your old sinful nature and your former way of life, which is corrupted by lust and deception. Instead, let the Spirit renew your thoughts and attitudes.'

Gal. 5:16 - 'So I say, let the Holy Spirit guide your lives. Then you won't be doing what your sinful nature craves.'

I pray God helps you come to grips with the reality of a life in Christ today, and I echo Paul's charge to you all:

'...Above all, you must live as citizens of heaven, conducting yourselves in a manner worthy of the Good News about Christ.' **(Phil. 1:27a)**

Have a blessed day! ^_^

Justice: A Short Meditation

I just wanted to share these cool verses I came across:

Prov. 24:23-25 - 'Here are some further sayings of the wise:
It is wrong to show favoritism when passing judgment. A judge who says to the wicked, "You are innocent," will be cursed by many people and denounced by the nations. But it will go well for those who convict the guilty; rich blessings will be showered on them.'

I find this passage amazing because it shows God's justice! It reminds me of our justification and how God could not simply just overlook our guilt, as under His law we were subject to death. 'In fact, according to the law of Moses, nearly everything was purified with blood. For without the shedding of blood, there is no forgiveness.' (Heb. 9:22)

People love talking about God's love and mercy, and rightly so, but these attributes do not then disregard His other attributes, such as His justice and holiness. Rather, it is when we take God in ALL of His character (as much as finite beings like us possible can), that we truly appreciate these attributes.

God's holiness requires us to abstain from sin (1 Pet. 1:16), and His justice requires all those who sin and go against His law to be subject to death (Rom. 5:12), yet His patience keeps Him from wiping us out (Rom. 2:4, Acts 17:30-31), His love sought to take up the cup of wrath that we deserved (Rom. 5:8), and His mercy counts us justified, not based on what we do or Him simply turning a blind eye, but because someone paid the price on our behalf; someone shed the blood for our atonement and fulfilled the requirements of the law (Eph. 2:4-6, Gal. 3:13, 2 Cor. 5:21).

It reminds me of the words of a hymn:

"Because the sinless Savior died,
My sinful soul is counted free,
For God the Just is satisfied,
To look on Him and pardon me." (Charitie Lees Bancroft, 'Before the Throne of God Above')

As we strive on to live our lives in light of the gospel, we continue to grasp the joy David expressed:

'Oh, what joy for those whose disobedience is forgiven, whose sin is put out of sight!' **(Ps. 32:1)**

I hope this message encourages you. Have a blessed day!

OLUFEMI IJAODOLA

Who Wants to Drink from a Dirty Spring?: A Short Meditation

I came across this ponder-worthy nugget of Scripture (well, they are ALL ponder-worthy in all fairness) and I thought to share it.

Proverbs 25:26

'If the godly give in to the wicked, it's like polluting a fountain or muddying a spring.' **(NLT)**

'Like a trampled spring and a polluted well is a righteous man who gives way before the wicked.' **(NASB)**

'A righteous man who falters before the wicked is like a murky spring and a polluted well.' **(NKJV)**

This is perhaps something we know but haven't considered with such imagery? (I know I hadn't until I read the verse).

The godly are meant to be an example to their unbelieving neighbors (Col. 4:5); they are to be as Christ —a refreshing well, spring or fountain which attracts those around them in this dry and thirsty land (the account of Jesus and the Samaritan woman in John 4:1-15 comes to mind).

As a point of contact in that sense, we have a responsibility to display rightly the faith we believe:

Prov. 13:14 - 'The instruction of the wise is like a life-giving fountain; those who accept it avoid the snares of death.' (cf. Prov. 9:10)

Matt. 5:13-16 - '"You are the salt of the earth. But what good is salt if it has lost its flavor? Can you make it salty again? It will be thrown out and trampled underfoot as worthless.
"You are the light of the world-like a city on a hilltop that cannot be hidden. No one lights a lamp and then puts it under a basket. Instead, a lamp is placed on a stand, where it gives light to everyone in the house.
In the same way, let your good deeds shine out for all to see, so that everyone will praise your heavenly Father.'

2 Cor. 5:19-20 - '...For God was in Christ, reconciling the world to Himself, no longer counting people's sins against them. And He gave us this wonderful message of reconciliation. So we are Christ's ambassadors; God is making His appeal through us. We speak for Christ when we plead, "Come back to God!"'

However, by neglecting the righteous path and giving in to sin, this refreshing spring is polluted and thus not attractive anymore. There is nothing attractive or refreshing about dirty water.

If you're like me (a human being), I'm sure you must have experienced the sorrow of falling short in front of others. However, I don't think we can excuse ourselves or pass on the blame for that. Like someone once said, "we are responsible for all of our failures, and none of our successes." (KB, 'I Can't Play the Background')

One act of hypocrisy seems to tarnish all that we might have said and done. People seem to focus more on the bad we do, as opposed to the good we do. 'As dead flies cause even a bottle of perfume to stink, so a little foolishness spoils great wisdom and honor.' (Ecc. 10:1)

With so many witnesses around us (some known to us, most

unknown), our actions are more far-reaching than we might think or understand. We must be careful about our conduct because not only do we live for One, but we live before many, and our lives might be the only 'bible' those around us get to read. We have to live as ambassadors of Christ, not by our own power or efforts, but by trusting God in our weaknesses and submitting to Him in our strengths.

The prayer is that they will be touched by our lives (which also happen to be our testimonies), and that they will then seek out Christ Jesus for themselves and know His goodness firsthand (John 4:39-42).

Professing to be a follower of Christ is a weighty responsibility, one which a lot of us—and all of us at some point—have taken far too lightly, and the sting of Paul's rebuke to the Romans can ache at the thought of that:

'You are so proud of knowing the law, but you dishonor God by breaking it. No wonder the Scriptures say, "The Gentiles blaspheme the name of God because of you."'
(Rom. 2:23-24)

God forbid that His name be trampled upon because of my inadequacy! He is beautiful and perfect, and if we fragile clay jars are willing to accept the call, the responsibility and the privilege to be His children, may He work in us and direct every step we take, that we might bring honor to His name by how we live.

Phil. 1:27a - 'Above all, you must live as citizens of heaven, conducting yourselves in a manner worthy of the Good News about Christ...'

Col. 3:17 - '...And whatever you do or say, do it as a representative of the Lord Jesus, giving thanks through Him to God the Father.'

I hope someone found this encouraging. Grace and peace to you all; have a good day! ^_^

OLUFEMI IJAODOLA

Trifling Thrills and Precious Promises: A Short Meditation

1 John 2:15-17 - 'Do not love this world nor the things it offers you, for when you love the world, you do not have the love of the Father in you. For the world offers only a craving for physical pleasure, a craving for everything we see, and pride in our achievements and possessions. These are not from the Father, but are from this world. And this world is fading away, along with everything that people crave. But anyone who does what pleases God will live forever.'

Ps. 34:9 - 'Fear the LORD, you His godly people, for those who fear Him will have all they need.'

2 Pet. 1:3-4 - 'By His divine power, God has given us everything we need for living a godly life. We have received all of this by coming to know Him, the one who called us to Himself by means of His marvelous glory and excellence.
And because of His glory and excellence, He has given us great and precious promises. These are the promises that enable you to share His divine nature and escape the world's corruption caused by human desires.'

All the world has to offer is an avenue to fulfill the temptations that come from our sinful nature (James 1:14-15), encouraging us to trade God's precious promises for the hollow thrills of the world.

2 Pet. 1:4 shows us that it is in light of knowledge of God's promises that we are able to escape the world's lies of fulfillment, and we can see this in our Lord Jesus' overcoming of His temptation by Satan in the desert (Matt. 4:1-11, James 4:7). He was flesh like we are (Matt. 26:41, Heb. 4:14-15), but He knew God's promises, and so He didn't buy in. Each time He resisted the Accuser. How? By the power of the Holy Spirit (Matt. 4:1, Rom. 8:11-16), and by the knowledge of the Word (Ps. 119:9-11, Ps. 119:105).

The Word of God is the full revelation of His nature and His promises to us (Ps. 19:7-11), and therefore the weapon we have to battle against temptations (Eph. 6:17).

I pray this exhortation has been edifying, and that when the lusting of this world whispers sweet temptation in your ears, you will remember the sweeter promises of God which have been fulfilled for all who are in Christ Jesus (Eph. 1:3-7, 2 Cor. 1:20-22).

Have a blessed day!

OLUFEMI IJAODOLA

The Weakness of My Heart: A Short Meditation

I don't know about you, but a lot of times I find myself putting on a brave face for others even when I feel like my heart is in pieces, or trying to be reassuring even though I have NO IDEA what is going to happen.

Now I know that a lot of people will be quick to respond, "yes, that's because I trust that God will work it all out," or something of that nature, and proceed to baptize me in Scriptures about it.

Don't get me wrong, I'm a strong believer of that; after all, the Bible DOES reassure us along those lines.
For example:

Ps. 27:5 - '...For He will conceal me there when troubles come; He will hide me in His sanctuary. He will place me out of reach on a high rock.'

Phil. 4:6-7 - 'Don't worry about anything; instead, pray about everything. Tell God what you need, and thank Him for all He has done. Then you will experience God's peace, which exceeds anything we can understand. His peace will guard your hearts and minds as you live in Christ Jesus.'

However, my purpose in writing this was to identify two ways in which we could go wrong in putting on our brave faces [perhaps I should have named this meditation that instead]:

1) Putting On a Brave Face for People

Coming clean, I admit there have been times when I have put on a brave face, in order to act like things didn't phase me. Looking back, I can only give credit to the pride within my own heart. I tried to come across as a strong and infallible Christian—ha! —one which was above reproach in my perspective of life. I tried to put on a brave face so that those who looked up to me or took account of my life (whoever they were) would look on me and be inspired at the way I took everything in my stride.

Worse yet, I convinced myself (as pride always makes you do) that I was doing it for THEIR GOOD! If they saw me not being phased by anything, then they too would not be phased by anything, and they would trust in God more...

...Yeah. If only I realized I was doing more harm than good. If only I realized that I was starting to sell the same dream people sold to me early in my Christian walk. The dream that if I came to Christ, everything would be okay, and I would live a serene and peaceful life.
How damaging is it to be drawn by a false promise of an easy life, only to find out that life is, in some respects, harder when you become a Christian?
Take a moment if you will, to think on this:

'Why am I discouraged? Why is my heart so sad? I will put my hope in God! I will praise Him again—my Savior and my God!' (Ps. 42:11)

Does that sound like someone with a brave face? No, not really. But does that sound like someone who doesn't trust in God? Definitely not! That sounds like someone wrestling with his weaknesses in order to steer his life with the truth.
I think it would be damaging to the Body of Christ if we carry on putting up a facade of strength, rather than

baring our weakness so that the strength of God might be made even more evident.

I recall being at an event a few years ago, and an acquaintance and fellow brother in Christ who was meant to perform got bad news that a family member had passed away. What did he do? He didn't put on a brave face and quote scriptures and carry on like nothing happened. He broke down in tears and worshiped the living God who holds our lives in His hands... And THEN went on to perform!

That account both inspired and convicted me about my confusion of strength, i.e. do I try and show MY strength or God's? Because if I was seeking to show God's strength, I wouldn't have any issues with revealing my own weaknesses (Disclaimer: wisdom and discernment are necessary):

2 Cor. 12:9b-10 - "'...My power works best in weakness." So now I am glad to boast about my weaknesses, so that the power of Christ can work through me. That's why I take pleasure in my weaknesses, and in the insults, hardships, persecutions, and troubles that I suffer for

Christ. For when I am weak, then I am strong.'

This brings me to the second point:

2) Putting On a Brave Face for God

Hahahaha. Each time I think about how I do this, I find it's folly both hilarious and saddening. What on earth or above could make me even presume to think that I can keep secrets from God, or fool Him?

'Even Death and Destruction hold no secrets from the LORD. How much more does He know the human heart!' (Prov. 15:11)

'...The LORD doesn't see things the way you see them. People judge by outward appearance, but the LORD looks at the heart."' (1 Sam. 16:7b)

'If we had forgotten the name of our God or spread our hands in prayer to foreign gods, God would surely have known it, for He knows the secrets of every heart.' (Ps. 44:20-21)

God sees the intentions and state of every heart. This is

one of the reasons why He is the only fit Judge, for He does not only take account of what you do, but also what you don't do!

Just to give an example of this, let's take a look at Jesus' teachings about anger and adultery:

Matt. 5:20-21 - '"You have heard that our ancestors were told, 'You must not murder. If you commit murder, you are subject to judgment.'
But I say, if you are even angry with someone, you are subject to judgment! If you call someone an idiot, you are in danger of being brought before the court. And if you curse someone, you are in danger of the fires of hell.'

Matt. 5:27-28 - '"You have heard the commandment that says, 'You must not commit adultery.' But I say, anyone who even looks at a woman with lust has already committed adultery with her in his heart...'

As we see, these sins were committed in the heart, even though they were not physically done, and so they were guilty of these sins, even though they had not actually carried them out!

But I digress...

What I'm trying to get at is that God sees the weakness of our hearts, so it makes no sense trying to put on a brave face before Him. He is our Friend, our Provider, and our God.
He is accustomed to our pain and sufferings, so why do we not lay our hearts before Him?

Do we think that He will judge us if we tell Him how we really feel?

Do we think that He would be none the wiser if we held back our struggles from Him?

Do we think that we would impress Him by not telling Him how much we struggle?

How can we ask for the strength and grace we need to get through, if we are not honest about the strength and grace we need to get through?

Jesus said, '..."Come to me, all of you who are weary and carry heavy burdens, and I will give you rest.' (Matt.

11:28)

Peter encourages, 'Give all your worries and cares to God, for He cares about you.' (1 **Pet. 5:7**)

The writer of Hebrews reveals the heart of God when he says:

'...So then, since we have a great High Priest who has entered heaven, Jesus the Son of God, let us hold firmly to what we believe. This High Priest of ours understands our weaknesses, for He faced all of the same testings we do, yet He did not sin.
So let us come boldly to the throne of our gracious God. There we will receive His mercy, and we will find grace to help us when we need it most.' (**Heb. 4:14-16**)

Going back to a verse I mentioned previously, we read:

'Don't worry about anything; instead, pray about everything. Tell God what you need, and thank Him for all He has done. Then you will experience God's peace, which exceeds anything we can understand. His peace will guard your hearts and minds as you live in Christ Jesus.' (Phil. 4:6-7)

Paul asks us to <u>tell</u> God what we need.

If you are wrestling with anger, <u>tell</u> God you're wrestling with anger, and ask Him to fill your heart with love and forgiveness. If you are struggling with unbelief, <u>tell</u> God you're struggling with unbelief, and ask Him to strengthen your faith with His Word of Truth. If you're anxious about your needs, <u>tell</u> God you're anxious about your needs, and ask Him to strengthen your trust in Him.

Most importantly, if you're caught in some sin, don't try to hide away and 'fix yourself up' before going to Him, but rather approach Him in humility and confess your weakness, repent of your sin and ask for His strength to serve Him in all reverence and fear.

Also, don't try and prove to the Lord that you're the best ChristIAN; remember, He is Christ.

So, I guess I just want to encourage you to be truthful with yourself. Don't muster up strength in yourself when you are weak, but rather admit your weakness and lean on God for strength.

I would like to end this meditation with this encouragement:

Ps. 27:7-10 - 'Hear me as I pray, O LORD. Be merciful and answer me!
My heart has heard You say, "Come and talk with Me." And my heart responds, "LORD, I am coming."
Do not turn Your back on me. Do not reject Your servant in anger. You have always been my helper. Don't leave me now; don't abandon me, O God of my salvation! Even if my father and mother abandon me, the LORD will hold me close.'

Have a blessed day! ^_^

Social Death?: A Short Meditation

Being a Christian, you inevitably become at odds with the world, simply because they revel in the evil practices that God dislikes, and you uphold a righteousness that they find disturbing, confusing, and convicting.

Jesus knew this quite well, so much so that He said this to His (then) unbelieving brothers:

'...The world cannot hate you, but it hates Me because I testify of it, that its deeds are evil.' (John 7:7, NASB)

The world embraces those who are in it. Bear in mind, however, that this doesn't mean they won't have their own troubles. It just means that they're more likely to 'fit in' and be accepted, than a follower of Christ is. We shouldn't be surprised then, if our friends or families don't approve of our new lives, or we get shunned and left out.

Jesus warned His disciples of the social death that came with believing and preaching the gospel:

'"If the world hates you, remember that it hated Me first. The world would love you as one of its own if you belonged to it, but you are no longer part of the world. I chose you to come out of the world, so it hates you. Do you remember what I told you? 'A slave is not greater than the master.' Since they persecuted Me, naturally they will persecute you. And if they had listened to Me, they would listen to you. They will do all this to you because of Me, for they have rejected the one who sent Me.' (John 15:18-21)

Those who genuinely follow Christ quickly come face to face with this, and the more we fight against this reality and seek acceptance, the more unproductive and unfruitful we become.

Why?

Because when trying to please both the world and God, we ultimately compromise on one side or the other... And God isn't one for half-heartedness:

'...Don't you realize that friendship with the world makes you an enemy of God? I say it again: If you want to be a friend of the world, you make yourself an enemy of God.' (James 4:4b)

Of course, this doesn't mean that you cannot or should not have unbelieving friends. After all, what's the point being a 'light' if you only stay around other 'lights', rather than going where the darkness is?

It is beneficial however to remember that if those friends were to turn against you, especially due to your faith in Christ Jesus, then you shouldn't be surprised, and you definitely shouldn't seek to compromise your faith on their account!

Paul knew of this reality when he wrote to the Galatians regarding a message that perhaps might not be the most attractive to hear:

'...Obviously, I'm not trying to win the approval of people, but of God. If pleasing people were my goal, I would not be Christ's servant.' (Gal. 1:10)

Now, what about the issue of families? Well, unfortunately, the same truth still applies. Whether related by blood or not, it still stands that you will probably not see eye-to-eye with them on a lot of things. As much as it sucks to be alienated in your own home, it could be the cost of choosing to follow Christ. However, 'to you who believe, He is precious' (1 Pet. 2:7), and definitely worth more than fitting in.

Jesus speaks about this fracture in relationships that might happen to His disciples:

'"Everyone who acknowledges Me publicly here on earth, I will also acknowledge before My Father in heaven. But everyone who denies Me here on earth, I will also deny before My Father in heaven.

"Don't imagine that I came to bring peace to the earth! I came not to bring peace, but a sword.

'I have come to set a man against his father, a daughter against her mother, and a daughter-in-law against her mother-in-law. Your enemies will be right in your own household!'

"If you love your father or mother more than you love Me, you are not worthy of being Mine; or if you love your son or daughter more than Me, you are not worthy of being Mine.' (Matt. 10:32-37)

...The cost is great, but nothing compared to knowing the Everlasting One, the Most High God!

'...For momentary, light affliction is producing for us an eternal weight of glory FAR BEYOND ALL COMPARISON,' (2 Cor. 4:17, NASB, emphasis added)

To end on a livelier note, even though you are likely to lose friends, and relationships will break because of this, you also gain new ones. For as we come to believe in Jesus Christ, we are adopted into God's own family:

'...As Jesus was speaking to the crowd, His mother and brothers stood outside, asking to speak to Him. Someone told Jesus, "Your mother and Your brothers are outside, and they want to speak to You."
Jesus asked, "Who is My mother? Who are My brothers?" Then He pointed to His disciples and said, "Look, these are My mother and brothers. Anyone who does the will of My Father in heaven is My brother and sister and mother!"' (Matt. 12:46-50)

For sake of this message not being too long, this is where we'll stop! I truly hope this encourages at least one of you. Have a blessed day! ^_^

God Loves You Anyway: A Short Meditation

Check out this stern passage:

Gal. 3:1-3 - 'Oh, foolish Galatians! Who has cast an evil spell on you? For the meaning of Jesus Christ's death was made as clear to you as if you had seen a picture of His death on the cross. Let me ask you this one question: Did you receive the Holy Spirit by obeying the law of Moses? Of course not! You received the Spirit because you believed the message you heard about Christ. How foolish can you be? After starting your Christian lives in the Spirit, why are you now trying to become perfect by your own human effort?'

Sometimes we get so caught up doing stuff, that we think we saved or cleansed ourselves (Prov. 20:9), or that God won't like us if we don't do this or do that. Yes, we are called to work out our salvation (Phil. 2:12) and abstain from things that might defile us (2 Cor. 7:1), but we must remember that it is Him doing the work in us (Phil. 1:6, Phil. 2:13, Heb. 12:1-3).

Understandably, we want to please God and so we strive to

do the things He desires for us. However, the problem is when we get so burdened by our own effort that our failures then become so damaging to our walks.

We must remember that God loved us while we were utterly helpless (Rom. 5:6) and still sinners (Rom. 5:8). If then, He loved us at our worst, why do we for some reason believe that He loves us any less now that we're striving to walk in the righteous path He has laid before us?

Ps. 37:23-24 - 'The LORD directs the steps of the godly. He delights in every detail of their lives. Though they stumble, they will never fall, for the LORD holds them by the hand.'

The above passage gives me comfort for many reasons, but for the sake of this meditation, we will focus on His delight. The LORD delights in the lives of the godly; He leads them in the path of righteousness for His name's sake (Ps. 23:3).

Matthew Henry comments about Ps. 37:24, "God will keep them from being ruined by their falls, either into sin or into trouble."

We are prone to wander and fall short of His glory, but rather than keeping our eyes on ourselves and our shortcomings, we should look at the One who saved us to begin with. Rather than wallowing in our weaknesses, we should glory in the strength of the LORD and the love by which He cleanses us and upholds us, even though we fall!

(Note: Our relationship with God should be Christ-centered, not me-centered.)

We should learn from Paul's harsh rebuke to the Galatians; we must not substitute the <u>fruit of our salvation</u> for the <u>reason for our salvation</u>. Faithful works are a result of His work in us, and not the reason He works in us, otherwise by that logic, we must have done something to cause Him to save us in the first place (Eph. 2:8-10)!

There is much more that can be said about all this, but the point I'm trying to get across is that we must not get so consumed by our doing stuff 'for God' to the point that we forget that we are not justified by them. Enjoy the fruits of a regenerate heart, but place more priority on seeing and savoring God, and trust that as you do so, the fruit of your salvation will be birthed out.

Phil. 1:9-11 - 'I pray that your love will overflow more and more, and that you will keep on growing in knowledge and understanding. For I want you to understand what really matters, so that you may live pure and blameless lives until the day of Christ's return. May you always be filled with the fruit of your salvation—the righteous character produced in your life by Jesus Christ—for this will bring much glory and praise to God.'

1 John 3:6 - 'Anyone who continues to live in Him will not sin. But anyone who keeps on sinning does not know Him or understand who He is.'

Have a blessed day brethren! ^_^

Don't Judge Me: A Short Meditation

I know most of us have probably heard (or more likely, said) one of these or a variation of them before:

"Don't judge me!"
"Who made you judge?!"
"Only God can judge me!'"
"You're so judgmental!"

With reason do I quote them with exclamation marks; almost ALL of the time, such things are said in defense of an action or attitude, but we will get to that later.

It seems common for us to remind those around us that they hold no higher authority than us, and so are in no place to pass any judgment. And funny enough, this mentality seems to have its basis in the Bible! I can identify at least these two verses in fact:

Matt. 7:1 - '"Do not judge so that you will not be judged.' (NASB)

John 8:7b - '...let the one who has never sinned throw the

first stone!"'

I think it would help to look at these verses a little closer.

The account in John 8:2-11 tells of the Pharisees bringing a woman 'caught in adultery' to Jesus for judgment. We note here that their intentions were not even for justice nor righteousness, but seeking fault and error in Jesus and His doctrine (v6). Quoting the law, they infer that those who are caught in sin should be put to death.
Following their reasoning then, it stands to say that only those who are without sin themselves would be in such standing as to pass such judgment, else they ought to be put to death themselves (Eze. 18:4, Jas. 2:10-11, Rom. 6:23a). Being far from blameless, none of them could meet the standard, and so relented.

This account beautifully ends with a picture of restoration, where Jesus graciously forgives the woman of her identified sin, and tells her to repent of it.
Now let's turn our attention to Matt. 7:1. We note here that the verse does not say, 'do not judge' and end it

there. In fact, I would say that to truly understand this verse, one must read on to at least v5. Jesus is saying that you will be judged by the same standard you use to judge others.

Many out of self-righteousness or hypocrisy are quick to find fault in others, yet are unable to (or choose not to) see their own faults. How can one who is blind tell another blind person that (s)he can lead the way? And how can you think of correcting someone when you indulge in even worse practices yourself?

Hypocrisy is a potent issue addressed in several places in the Bible.

Rom. 2:1-3 is one that similarly talks about judgment. In the previous chapter Paul had listed some depraved practices that the world indulges in, and then as if predicting the self-righteous pride that would swell up in the readers, addresses it:

Rom. 2:1-3 - '...You may think you can condemn such people, but you are just as bad, and you have no excuse! When you say they are wicked and should be punished, you are condemning yourself, for you who judge others do these very same things. And we know that God, in His justice, will punish anyone who does such things. Since you judge others for doing these things, why do you think you can avoid God's judgment when you do the same things?'

Okay, so we can start to see a picture forming here (I hope). In the instances usually referred to that I mentioned above, what was being rejected was not judgment itself, but rather the hypocritical attitude of double-standards, and the self-righteous attitude of seeing all the fault in others and none of the ones in yourself.

However, does this mean that one cannot judge between right and wrong? Of course not! After all, even if we ignore the fact that we pass judgment about things that are right and wrong daily, and even if we ignore that our consciences also pass such judgments on our behalf (Rom. 2:14-15), what would be the point in God revealing His heart and pleasure to us, if we do not use that knowledge to inform our actions and attitudes (Rom. 12:2)?

Now, here we will split it into two: judgment in the midst

of believers and unbelievers.

All those who come to Christ and make the decision to live their lives in line with His will are called to the same glorious standard:

'...So you must live as God's obedient children. Don't slip back into your old ways of living to satisfy your own desires. You didn't know any better then. But now you must be holy in everything you do, just as God who chose you is holy. For the Scriptures say, "You must be holy because I am holy."' (1 Pet. 1:14-16)

To see a fellow brother or sister slipping into sin and not correct them is neither caring nor loving. We are called to show them love by correction, using the same standard which we are ALL called to (notice here that this does not contradict the points made above, as not only is the motive here restoration and love, but it is judgment in full light of the fact that we are also held accountable to the same standard).

Here are some instances of this:

Jas. 5:19-20 - 'My dear brothers and sisters, if someone among you wanders away from the truth and is brought back, you can be sure that whoever brings the sinner back will save that person from death and bring about the forgiveness of many sins.'

Gal. 6:1 - 'Dear brothers and sisters, if another believer is overcome by some sin, you who are godly should gently and humbly help that person back onto the right path. And be careful not to fall into the same temptation yourself.'

1 Thess. 5:14-15 - 'Brothers and sisters, we urge you to warn those who are lazy. Encourage those who are timid. Take tender care of those who are weak. Be patient with everyone. See that no one pays back evil for evil, but always try to do good to each other and to all people.'

We can see from these examples that the 'judgment' here is one of identifying sin, and correcting one another in love, not condemnation. In some respect, this is easier as all in Christ take the Scriptures as the highest authority (or at least they ought to), and so we all refer to the same standard.

Now on to the unbelieving. Paul writes to the Corinthian Church:

'It isn't my responsibility to judge outsiders, but it certainly is your responsibility to judge those inside the church who are sinning.
God will judge those on the outside; but as the Scriptures say, "You must remove the evil person from among you."' (1 Cor. 5:12-13)

We see here that while Christians are urged to pass judgment on sin (and by that I mean identify and correct it, not condemn those caught up in it, nor ignore it), it is God who will judge those who do not believe (well, it is God who judges all anyway).
So then, does this justify the saying, 'only God can judge me?'

Well... yes and no.

True, we cannot hold others accountable to a standard they neither accept nor agree with; only God can hold them to His standard Himself, since He requires all men to be upright. However, we can evangelize and bear witness to God's love to all.

I propose that when we see an unbeliever caught up in sin, we do not turn away and say, "well only God can judge him/her". Rather, we use that as an opportunity to share the Gospel in love, praying that God has mercy on the person so that (s)he can come to a point of conviction and repentance. After all, before one can turn away from sin, one must first admit that (s)he is a sinner! And we cannot expect the fruit of salvation from one that has not experienced salvation to begin with.

Now, the last point I want to address before we conclude is my earlier statement about the statement mostly used in defense.

Have you noticed that whenever you praise someone's actions or attitude, they do not respond, "don't judge me"? Well of course they wouldn't! That is because you are judging them favorably. This hints at a point: judgment seems to only become a problem when it is unfavorable or corrective!!

And with that, we will stop here. As usual, there is a lot more that can be said about this, but I hope you at least had an enjoyable read!

May God help us ALL to put away our hypocrisy, and help us to not be speakers alone of the Word, but doers also! (You see the spin there? ^_^)

[Disclaimer: If you read this and feel that I am judging or that I cannot judge you, then I assure you that it wasn't my intention to come across judgmental, but I pose to you this question: Why do you feel judged?]

Eph. 5:10-11 - 'Carefully determine what pleases the Lord. Take no part in the worthless deeds of evil and darkness; instead, expose them.'

OLUFEMI IJAODOLA

The Challenger: A Short Meditation

Jesus gave an illustration of the clash of powers:

Matt. 12:29 - '...For who is powerful enough to enter the house of a strong man like Satan and plunder his goods? Only someone even stronger—someone who could tie him up and then plunder his house.'

So, unless the challenger is stronger, (s)he would not succeed... Taking this precedence, let's look at another statement about power Jesus made:

John 10:28-29 - 'My sheep listen to My voice; I know them, and they follow Me. I give them eternal life, and they will never perish. No one can snatch them away from Me, for my Father has given them to Me, and He is more powerful than anyone else. No one can snatch them from the Father's hand.'

So, putting these two illustrations together and flipping it around, unless the challenger is stronger than God and able to 'tie Him up', (s)he is unable to plunder His house. However, Jesus perishes that argument by clearly asserting, '...He is more powerful than anyone else.'

No one can plunder His house because no one is able to tie Him up. No one can snatch us out of His hand because no one is able to stay His hand.

Dan. 4:35 - 'All the peoples of the earth are regarded as nothing. He does as He pleases with the powers of heaven and the peoples of the earth. No one can hold back His hand or say to Him: "What have You done?"' **(ESV)**

Isa. 40:25 - '"To whom will You compare me? Who is My equal?" asks the Holy One.'

So we see then, that since it would take someone stronger than Him to thwart His will (and we know that there is NONE like or greater than Him), it means His will can never be thwarted!

That makes Paul's conviction all the more convincing:

'...And I am convinced that nothing can ever separate us from God's love. Neither death nor life, neither angels nor demons, neither our fears for today nor our worries about tomorrow—not even the powers of hell can separate us from God's love.

No power in the sky above or in the earth below—indeed,

nothing in all creation will ever be able to separate us from the love of God that is revealed in Christ Jesus our Lord.' (Rom. 8:38-39)

So, be encouraged; nothing can stop what the Most High God has in-store for you. If He decrees it, so it shall be (Isa. 46:10). With the wealth of promises He has given us, and the culmination of all goodness He has granted us in Christ, we can be assured that HIS LOVE IS REAL, and indeed, it is an unstoppable force, and an unquenchable flame! All opposition, all anxieties, all insecurities; all are swallowed up in victory by His love for us.

"We are secure, not because we hold tightly to Jesus, but because He holds tightly to us." - R.C. Sproul

'Give thanks to the Lord, for He is good,
for His steadfast love endures forever.
Give thanks to the God of gods,
for His steadfast love endures forever.
Give thanks to the Lord of lords,
for His steadfast love endures forever;' (Ps. 136:1-3, ESV)

Rest in His love today, and have a blessed day! ^_^

To-Morrow: A Short Meditation

I was just thinking about plans and life and whatnot, and two passages came to mind, so thought to share them with a little encouragement:

Matt. 6:31-33 - '...Do not worry then, saying, 'What will we eat?' or 'What will we drink?' or 'What will we wear for clothing?' For the Gentiles eagerly seek all these things; for your heavenly Father knows that you need all these things. But seek first His kingdom and His righteousness, and all these things will be added to you.' **(NASB)**

This passage instructs us not to be anxious about provisions nor what tomorrow holds, for God knows our needs. Notice that it doesn't say that we no longer have needs because we are saved, but rather as children of God we have the confidence that He _knows_ our needs, so we shouldn't be worried about whether or not He will provide for them.

There are higher and better things to strive for, while trusting that He will indeed open His hand and satisfy our desires in due season (Ps. 145:14-17).

And so we move on to the second passage:

Jas. 4:14-16 - 'Come now, you who say,
"Today or tomorrow we will go to such and such a city, and spend a year there and engage in business and make a profit."
Yet you do not know what your life will be like tomorrow. You are just a vapor that appears for a little while and then vanishes away. Instead, you ought to say, "If the Lord wills, we will live and also do this or that."' **(NASB)**

Unlike the first passage which encourages about not being anxious about tomorrow, this passage is almost at the opposite side of the spectrum, warning against over-confidence about tomorrow.

There is nothing wrong with making plans, and it is indeed wise to do so, but such plans must <u>always</u> be committed before the LORD.

Apart from avoiding putting confidence in ourselves, this is also a blessed thing to do because He delights in guiding us in the right path, and He is our only security (Ps. 37:23-25), so it is hard to reason why any plans we make would be devoid of Him.

And if that doesn't encourage you to willingly trust and submit all your plans, actions and desires to Him, then maybe His sovereignty will, for:

'We can make our plans, but the LORD determines our steps' (Prov. 16:19),

and

'You can make many plans, but the LORD's purpose will prevail.' (Prov. 19:21)

So there you have it... I hope these short passages (and unexpectedly long commentary) will serve as an encouragement, as well as challenge your perspectives on planning.

I would encourage further studying when you can; prayerfully get into the Scriptures, and ask God for a godly perspective on this and indeed all things... God knows we all need to renew our minds and thinking!

Have a blessed day ^_^

If You Have Been Raised Up...: A Short Meditation

Col. 3:1-4 - '...Therefore if you have been raised up with Christ, keep seeking the things above, where Christ is, seated at the right hand of God. Set your mind on the things above, not on the things that are on earth. For you have died and your life is hidden with Christ in God. When Christ, who is our life, is revealed, then you also will be revealed with Him in glory.' (NASB)

While going through this passage at a Church gathering, a pastor made a comment about a beautiful truth. He referred to this passage as one of the assurances we have in the doctrine of 'once saved, always saved'.

If the life of the believer is indeed 'hidden with Christ in God' (and Christ is even now 'our life', cf. Gal. 2:20), then it means it cannot be lost nor stolen. As none can pluck those who are His out of His hands, then it is hard to imagine a child of God losing his/her life to something that Christ died to redeem him/her from, ONCE FOR ALL TIME.

Of course, by no means does this allow for an abuse of grace by the believer (as a true believer ought not to be comfortable with disobeying the God (s)he professes to serve), but it means that there is no condemnation for those who are in Christ (Rom. 8:1); only godly convictions (2 Cor. 7:8-10), a sense of dissatisfaction with our current state (Ps. 42:1-2), and a desire to be conformed more to the image of our Lord with each passing day (Phil. 3:12-14).

So as an encouragement, if indeed you have been 'raised up with Christ', be assured that even though you might fall, He is working in you and WILL bring His work to completion (Phil. 1:6), and know that the One who promises these things is faithful to keep His promises (1 Thess. 5:23-24, Heb. 10:23).

If indeed you profess to believe in Christ and are working towards surrendering <u>all</u> aspects of your life to Him, but yet find yourself in a cycle/habit of sinning, ask Him to convict you of it and lead you to repentance; His salvation is not at a future date, but now!

And if you find that you have been straddling the fence; you find the joys in Christ appealing, but can't seem to commit your life to Him, then I would encourage taking time out to ask Him to help you make that decision. After all, if nothing is worth more than your soul (Mark 8:37), then what sort of worth could you even attempt to attach to the One who created it? And if He is beyond any value we might attempt to attach to Him, then why wouldn't you want Him?

1 Pet. 2:24-25 - '...and He Himself bore our sins in His body on the cross, so that we might die to sin and live to righteousness; for by His wounds you were healed. For you were continually straying like sheep, but now you have returned to the Shepherd and Guardian of your souls.' **(NASB)**

He is the kind of Shepherd that leaves the 99 to retrieve the 1... Those sheep who were once lost but now found cannot be lost again under His watch; He is not a hired hand that abandons the sheep when things don't go according to plan (John 10:11-13).

And if you are still straying away, being led astray by empty promises of greener pastures, then...

"Come back home, you lost sheep." (Aszerina Ijaodola, 'Lost Sheep')

Desires & Temptations: A Short Meditation

"Indeed, if we consider the unblushing promises of reward and the staggering nature of the rewards promised in the Gospels, it would seem that Our Lord finds our desires, not too strong, but too weak. We are half-hearted creatures, fooling about with drink and sex and ambition when infinite joy is offered us, like an ignorant child who wants to go on making mud pies in a slum because he cannot imagine what is meant by the offer of a holiday at the sea. We are far too easily pleased." - **C.S. Lewis, 'The Weight of Glory'**

I wonder why temptations feel so hard to ignore. I understand that the flesh is weak and all, but why isn't it easy to just look away? After all, I believe most of the time we KNOW that what we're being tempted to do/say is evil (or at least inappropriate), and on a normal day, I don't think anyone consciously sets out to be evil (unless you're a super villain).

This passage comes to mind:

'Let no one say when he is tempted, "I am being tempted

by God," for God cannot be tempted with evil, and He Himself tempts no one. But each person is tempted when he is lured and enticed by his own desire. Then desire when it has conceived gives birth to sin, and sin when it is fully grown brings forth death.' (James 1:13-15, ESV)

According to this, we are tempted by our OWN desires. This means a part of us actually WANTS to do or say that particular thing, and that's why the temptation seems so appealing. After all, what's the point using a bait that the prey has no interest in? If we were being tempted by something we had no desire for, then it wouldn't be temptation!

I cannot speak for everyone, but I personally find it frustrating that even after coming to Christ, there are still these 'desires' lurking in my heart that can so easily tempt me to go astray.
Although I would speculate that the root of it all can be called the 'sin issue' (we are all fallen, and even when redeemed, still reside in this imperfect body of weakness until the day He returns), or the 'worship issue' (all sin is a

disregard for God's Word and who He is, hence a result of a lack of proper view and reverence of Him); in the midst of those are various motives and desires that could lead one to sin.

For example, one could partake in theft or fraud or other illegal activities out of a desire to obtain/retain more money (e.g. in the case of tax evasion), or it could be out of a desire to prove that he/she could do these things and get away with it. Even yet, the desire could be something less greedy, like having dependents and not having 'enough' to meet their needs.

Either way, when the 'opportunity' presents itself, it is likely to be a desirous course of action (or at least an action leading to a desirous result), and hence, a temptation.
Money here is a common example, but it can easily be applied to other situations and sins such as lying, sexual immorality, pride, murder, etc.

The desires that lead to temptation do not have to be inherently bad for it to lead to sin. Examples of this could be someone who desires to get ahead in his job—which isn't wrong—but steals his colleague's ideas to do so; or a lady who is engaged, desiring to get married and consummate, which isn't wrong, but becoming impatient and ending up fornicating with her husband-to-be.

As you have seen, these 'temptations' don't have to spring from evil desires or intentions; they could just as easily be the pull to fulfil a legitimate desire in an evil or inappropriate way, as shown above.
(Take note, you who are fond of saying, "the end justifies the means"!)

So how is a follower of Christ supposed to deal with these desires?

The Bible talks about things like 'renewing your mind' (Rom. 12:2, Eph. 4:23), 'putting off' of old selves and 'putting on' of new selves (Col. 3:5-13, Eph. 4:20-24), and 'working out' your salvation (Phil. 2:12-13).

In truth, the Word of God contains much encouragement on the process of getting our hearts in line with His will (which is commonly called 'sanctification', being 'set apart', or being made 'holy'), and I will try to summarize it all into four simple points:

1) <u>Remember who God is</u> (e.g. Deut. 7:9-10, Ps. 103:1-6, 1 Pet. 1:15-16)

2) <u>Remember who we now are in Him</u> (e.g. Col. 3:1-4, 1 John 3:1-3, 2 Cor. 6:14-18)

3) <u>Remember who we were before coming to Him</u> (e.g. Rom. 6:20-21, Eph. 2:11-12)

4) <u>Remember what it took to get us from 3) to 2)</u> (e.g. Gal. 3:13-14, 2 Cor. 5:21, 1 Pet. 2:24-25)

...Wow, okay I just realized I am getting a bit too broad beyond what I wanted to say.

Right, to conclude...

When temptation comes your way, do not feel helpless and powerless to its urges. For all those in Christ are no longer slaves to sin; He put an end to that on the cross:

Rom. 6:10-13 - '...For the death that He died, He died to sin once for all; but the life that He lives, He lives to God. Even so consider yourselves to be dead to sin, but alive to God in Christ Jesus. Therefore do not let sin reign in your mortal body so that you obey its lusts, and do not go on presenting the members of your body to sin as instruments of unrighteousness; but present yourselves to God as those alive from the dead, and your members as instruments of righteousness to God.' **(NASB)**

So, when you feel tempted, you don't have to try to overcome by your own strength [that likely won't work anyway]. You have a High Priest who understands what you are going through, and is able to help you:

Heb. 2:16-18 - '...For assuredly He does not give help to angels, but He gives help to the descendant of Abraham. Therefore, He had to be made like His brethren in all things, so that He might become a merciful and faithful high priest in things pertaining to God, to make propitiation for the sins of the people. For since He Himself was tempted in that which He has suffered, He is able to come to the aid of those who are tempted.' **(NASB)**

Heb. 4:14-16 - 'Therefore, since we have a great high priest who has passed through the heavens, Jesus the Son of God, let us hold fast our confession. For we do not have a high priest who cannot sympathize with our weaknesses, but One who has been tempted in all things as we are, yet without sin.
Therefore let us draw near with confidence to the throne of grace, so that we may receive mercy and find grace to help in time of need.' **(NASB)**

And if you do fall to temptation, He intercedes on your behalf, and there is 'no condemnation for those in Christ Jesus' (Rom. 8:1), so confess your sin, repent, and strive for faithful obedience.

1 John 1:9 - 'If we confess our sins, He is faithful and just to forgive us our sins and to cleanse us from all unrighteousness.' **(ESV)**

Undoubtedly, all this has only scratched the surface, and I would encourage you to dig into the Word yourselves and study; not only to increase your knowledge of the One you serve, but also to help your love for Him grow to the extent that your appetite for His goodness destroys your appetite for sin. All this is by His strength though, and by His grace He will help us rid ourselves of sinful desires, as well as teach us trust in Him and discipline to deal with those right desires which we are tempted to fulfill sinfully.

Stand firm my brothers and sisters, and know that He doesn't abandon you when you're being tempted; He is with you, just as He has always been:

1 Cor. 10:13 - 'No temptation has overtaken you but such as is common to man; and God is faithful, who will not allow you to be tempted beyond what you are able, but with the temptation will provide the way of escape also, so that you will be able to endure it.' **(NASB)**

MAY THE MEDITATIONS OF MY HEART…

OLUFEMI IJAODOLA

MAY THE MEDITATIONS OF MY HEART…

Poetry

OLUFEMI IJAODOLA

MAY THE MEDITATIONS OF MY HEART...

A Restful Thought

Such angst about what tomorrow holds,

But then I stopped and prayed;

Be it glad tidings or sorrow's load,

In Christ my heart is stayed.

Your love endures on this fading stage:

My hope I'll reach the goal—

When winds come roaring and billows rage,

—An anchor for the soul.

Things might not work as I desire,

But surely as You plan;

Though now being molded through the fire,

Still safely in Your hand.

Teach me to trust when I cannot see,

With faith that You are there;

You support my lot, Lord, let it be

On Christ I cast my cares.

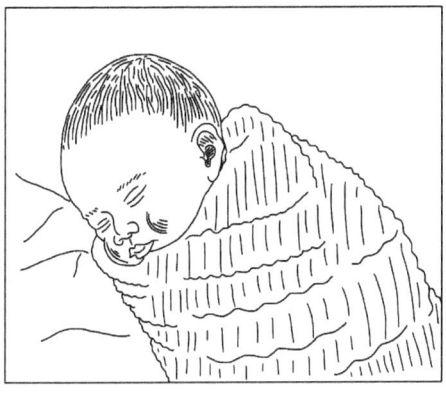

Christ-Mass

'Hark! The herald angels sing,

"Glory to the newborn King!"'

The crowds amass to celebrate the birth of a child,

So small, so weak, so tender, and mild.

The world looked on, awestruck in wonder;

Could this be the One who fixes our blunder?

He had no splendor, no riches, no fame;

So unexpected was the manner He came.

Began His ministry so late in His life,

The carpenter's son now claims to be Christ?

He spoke with such wisdom, such knowledge, such power;

None was greater, His anointing towered.
Miracles followed everywhere He went;
"The Kingdom is at hand, ye sinners, repent!"

Causing a ruckus now, the Pharisees hated this,
So they plotted a way to make His tongue cease.
The plan was set; they would capture this Jesus;
The price for betrayal? Simple, thirty pieces.

The Cup of wrath awaited Him, filled like a flood;
In such agony now, sweating drops of His blood;
If God would allow, let the cup pass over the Son;
Nonetheless, let God's will be done.

Tried and found innocent, but condemned anyway,
The Lamb of God was led to be slain.
Hung on the tree on the hill at Golgotha,
The Son was crushed, and it pleased the Father.

So Life itself tasted death and was laid in the grave,
But rose on the third day; God is mighty to save!
The Gospel of Christ spread throughout the earth:
The Messiah did come, as prophesied, a virgin birth.

Christmas is a time of remembrance of when our Savior came,
But we Christians celebrate this every single day.
So prepare the funeral dirge, and compose the wedding tune;
Maranatha, Maranatha; our Lord is coming soon!

Sin no longer has a hold, death no longer has its sting,
Until Christ returns, I join with the saints and I sing:
'Nothing in my hand, I bring...
Simply to the cross I cling.'

Untitled

Oh pitiful soul in sorrows dwelt,

Whence forth is thine anguish felt?

Hope in the LORD, again, rejoice!

Harden not thy heart, harken to His voice,

The sweet waters that wash away pain

Deeply felt, but never again.

Trust in the LORD who keeps thee safe,

And dwell with Him always, in the secret place.

Mountains may crumble, oceans may rise,

But hope in the One who hears thy cries.

My wits may fail me, my emotions lead astray,

But with trust in Christ Jesus, all will be okay.

Selah.

Maybe Someday

If we say Christmas is about trees,

I would assume we were talking about the one which He was hung upon,

Accursed to save you and me...

If we say Christmas is about gifts and presents,

I would think we imply how God graced us with His presence,

Forgiveness through Jesus Christ, and knowing Him: eternal life...

If we say Christmas is about family,

I would interrupt to confirm we meant His adoption of

rebels,
'Cause when the dust settled, we were named His after Calvary...

If we conclude then, that Christmas is about love,
Oh yes, it would be my pleasure to agree!
After all, what else could move a blameless man to die for a wretch like me?

Why be so caught up with decorating a tree, when you could ponder how the Creator of life put on flesh, just to relate to you and me, and to show us we're not alone?

Why be so occupied about gifts and presents,
When He promises you His treasures, and better yet,
Himself as your inheritance,
If you would let Him make your hearts His home?

I think if we got over the novelty of nativity scenes, then we would see; It isn't all as it seems.
How else could you explain how quickly we glance over GOD BECOMING A BABY?

Becoming like us just so He could die in our place, pay for OUR sin, with HIS grace? Crazy.

But perhaps these things are too lofty to think about while munching on chicken and chilling out...
Perhaps I'll just see it as a celebration of God's Son's birthday and remember He was born for my sake,
And look past the new games console and flashing lights,
Past the hand-knitted scarfs and hearty laughs,
Past this custard and cake I have on my plate,
Past the sea of snacks and luscious food,
And add thanksgiving to my merry mood;
And hope and pray, that God would make me understand all this a lot better someday.
Ah yes, I'll hope and I'll pray... Who knows, maybe even today.

I'm Upset.

I'm upset. I'm quite upset.

Upset with myself, upset with you; upset at the world.

So upset that I'm writing poetry that doesn't even seem to rhyme.

Why won't it rhyme?!

Well, I guess this won't be the first time.

So why am I upset, you ask?

I guess I'm upset at the state of the world.

It's quite depressing, isn't it?

So much suffering, so much pain...

It doesn't seem to stop; these tears that rain.

And I've been told the cause of the state we're in:

A 3-letter word, we call it 'sin'.

Get Behind Me

Oh, how you play with my senses!

You made me divorce wisdom and break down my fences of self-control;

Convincing me only you can make me whole.

Oh, how you play with my emotions;

Blindingly led down the path you desired for me, you stole my devotion, you fiend!

Assuring me you had all that I need.

Oh, how you play with my time!

Minutes and hours racked up in servitude;

Misery for gratitude,

OLUFEMI IJAODOLA

I'm so sick of your crimes!

Oh, how you obscure my vision;
My mission forgotten, thoughts marred up and rotten,
His Word turned echoes, turned slur.

But then, my memory stirs...
I remember the lens that focused the image of love, grace and mercy once blurred.
I remember the One who redeemed me, and urged me also to redeem my time;
Indeed, I remember He who pardoned my crimes.
I remember the Bridge over the chasm of failure and ineptitude I could never get over;
Indeed, I remember the rolled boulder.

Oh, how I see you clearer now!
You try to tempt me out of my vows with promises of better pleasure;
Like you could surpass His love poured out without measure!

Oh, I rebuke you now, get behind me;

When Christ hung on that tree, you were laid aside.

You will never again separate my Love and I.

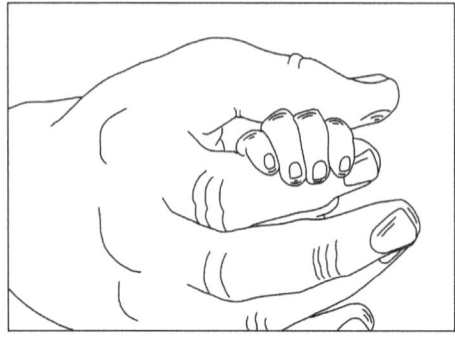

Nothing More

When the enemy stalks you like a prowler,

Lays his snares in wait like a fowler,

And fears have made your drink turn sour;

This could be the deadliest hour!

But in the LORD is a strong tower,

One who holds all the power

To turn thunderstorms to blessed showers—

The glory His; the victory ours!

So when you walk through the shadow of death,

And you feel like there's no hope left,

Trust the One who supplies your breath;

Oh Rock of Ages, won't You cleft?

See, we know not the height nor depth,

Of the love of Him who walked the earth

He created, our weight of sin to heft,

And to give new life; a second birth.

Now we have joy and peace galore;

If we have Jesus, we need nothing more.

This world's distractions turn to bore

When we grasp what God has in-store.

He placed eternity in our core,

So He'd be the One we'd grope for.

Now we have joy and peace galore,

If we have Jesus; we need nothing more.

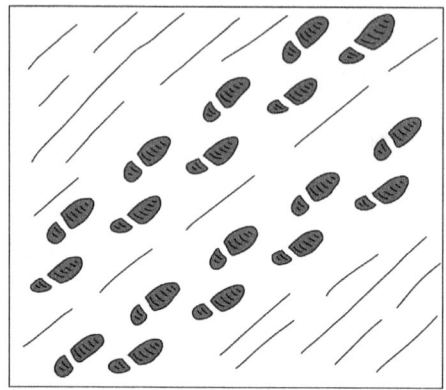

Are We There Yet?

This journey has gone on longer than I thought;

The scenery gets repetitive and leaves a lot to be desired.

I'm hungry. I'm frustrated. I'm tired—

Are we there yet?

Why are we taking the long way round?

Look, those people are taking a shortcut;

I know only You know the way to where we're going, but

Are we there yet?

Please, can we stop for a second?

The weather is unforgiving; a moment's peace is hard to find.

I need a while here to steady my mind, or

Are we there yet?

I need something to keep me going;

I find my steps losing their zeal;

This narrow and buffeted road has no appeal...

Are we there yet?

Ah.

I can't go on anymore; just let it be;

This journey was always too hard for me.

I left Egypt to be with You; I tried my best,

But I fear I'm to perish in this wilderness.

I can't go back the way I came,

But still can't see the better country which You claim.

Maybe I'll gather some sticks and stones,

Pile them up to make my home,

Dig a hole and hope it rains,

And play some games to ease the pain.

Farewell then, I'm off to play...

But still... Why do You stay?

I'm stopping here; don't You understand?
Why won't You let go of my hand?
I don't know what You want me to do;
I have no strength left to follow You.

Oh, You say You'll hold me up?
Okay, but don't blame me if the going gets tough.
You say You're strong enough and You'll be fine?
All right; the load is Yours to bear, not mine.

Ah.

I dare say, it's a little easier to walk this way;
Why didn't You suggest this from the first day?
You say You wanted me to get to my end,
To show that I'd have no better Friend?

Well, what a friend You are!
Thank You for it all; I'm forever in Your debt.
Now I hope You don't mind me asking...
Are we there yet?

Forgive me; You know I'm fickle and weak,
And I trust You appreciate me being frank when I speak,

So for now I'll share all my worries and cares,

And trust that You'll tell me when we get there.

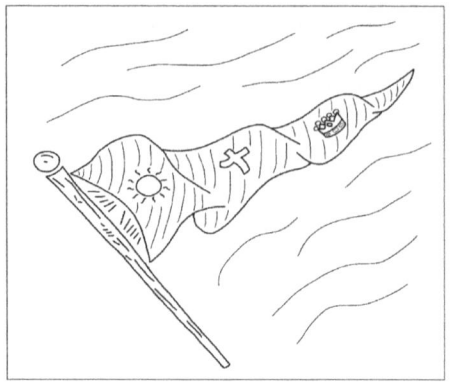

Receive Us

1. To think in eternity

Past, the holy Trinity

In Their pleasure, thought of me;

Scarcely can I contain!

Ev'n before my evil deeds,

He knew my salvific need,

Priceless price, He had to bleed;

The Lamb of God was slain!

Reprise:

For wretched men You died,

Now Lord, be glorified.

Help Your children come alive

And lay hold of this freedom!
Tempted much, on every side,
But grace abounding, every time;
Your mercies Lord have multiplied,
Receive us in Your kingdom!

2. Onward bound, no time for rest;
This prize of Your righteousness
Enflames our souls; onward, Yes!
We must finish the race.
Forsaking all these worldly things,
What lust and fleshly pleasures bring;
Our main goal now: to please the King,
And meet Him face to face!

Reprise:
For wretched men You died,
Now Lord, be glorified.
Help Your children come alive
And lay hold of this freedom!
Tempted much, on every side,
But grace abounding, every time;

Your mercies Lord have multiplied,
Receive us in Your kingdom!

3. But could it be, we would forget?
The late night cries and early weeping,
For in Your hands, to be held and kept,
And think that now, our God is sleeping?
Help us Lord to regard the cost;
The life You gave up on that cross;
To know You: gain, and all else loss;
This earth is not our home!

Reprise:
For wretched men You died,
Now Lord, be glorified.
Help Your children come alive
And lay hold of this freedom!
Tempted much, on every side,
But grace abounding, every time;
Your mercies Lord have multiplied,
Receive us in Your kingdom!

----

www.ingramcontent.com/pod-product-compliance
Lightning Source LLC
LaVergne TN
LVHW051517070426
835507LV00023B/3166